AF609474

HARYANA

A STATE STUDY GUIDE

J. S. SEHRAWAT

Published by

Hawk Press
4836/24, Ansari Road, Daryaganj
New Delhi – 110 002
Phones: 91-11-23278618, 91-11-43667199
E-mail: thehawkpress@gmail.com
www.thehawkpress.com

ISBN: 978-93-88318-72-3

Preface

Haryana, the land of great Epic Mahabharata fame, has had a glorious history. A small state of India, Haryana played vital role in India's freedom struggle. The modern Haryana has made great strides in the field of agricultural production and dairy development. Haryana is the 17th state of India that came into being on 1st November 1966 and presently has 22 districts. Previously it was under Punjab. It is situated in the North Western region surrounded by Himachal Pradesh from North, Uttrakhand from North East, Rajasthan from the South, U.P and Delhi from East and Punjab from North West. The largest district of Haryana is Bhiwani while Panchkula is the smallest district. Panchkula, along with Mohali and Chandigarh is called Tricity.

Haryana's culture is reflective of this colourful state. Submerged in the rich cultural heritage of Vedic Period, the mystical state of Haryana stands out from the crowd. Characterised by the hookahs and the charpoys, the vivid fairs and the swaying paddy fields; Haryana is one of the wealthiest states in India and is one of the most economically developed regions in South Asia. Popularly known as 'The Home of Gods', Haryana shares its borders with Rajasthan, Uttar Pradesh, Punjab, Himachal Pradesh and Delhi. This vibrant state has a bountiful culture, heritage, festivals, folklores and a vibrant landscape.

The total area of the state is 17,070 sq miles or 44,212 km2 which makes it the 20th biggest state in India by area. As laid down by the census performed in 2011, the population of the state is 27,761,063, making it the 16th most populated state in India. The density of population in Haryana is 1,485.212/ sq miles or 573.443/km^2.

Woodlands cover a total area of 1,553 km^2 of the state. The variety of flora in the state includes eucalyptus, mulberry, kikar, pine, babul and shisham. A wide variety of fauna is seen in Haryana comprising nilgai, blackbuck, fox, panther, jackal, mongoose, and wild dog. Over 300 varieties of birds are seen in the state.

The literacy rate of the state is 76.4% and the state occupies the 17th position in India in terms of literacy. About 90% of the population of the state are Hindus, 6.2% are Sikhs, 0.10% Christians, and 4.05% are Muslims. In addition, there are a small number of Jains living in the state. The official language of the state is Hindi. Other languages spoken in the state include Haryanvi, Sanskrit, English, Punjabi and Ahirwati.

Industries like business process outsourcing (BPO), manufacturing, retail and agriculture are the backbone of the state's economy. Service industries also make a significant contribution to the economic development of the state.

This is a reference book. All the matter is just compiled and edited in nature, taken from the various sources which are in public domain.

The present book encompasses authoritative information on the past history, society, culture and economy. These topics are categorically discussed in modern context too.

—*Editor*

ABOUT THE BOOK

Haryana, the land of great Epic Mahabharata fame, has had a glorious history. A small state of India, Haryana played vital role in India's freedom struggle. The modern Haryana has made great strides in the field of agricultural production and dairy development. Haryana is the 17th state of India that came into being on 1st November 1966 and presently has 22 districts. Previously it was under Punjab. It is situated in the North Western region surrounded by Himachal Pradesh from North, Uttrakhand from North East, Rajasthan from the South, U.P and Delhi from East and Punjab from North West. The largest district of Haryana is Bhiwani while Panchkula is the smallest district. Panchkula, along with Mohali and Chandigarh is called Tricity. Indian traditions regard this region as the matrix of creation of northern altar' where Brahma performed the pristine sacrifice and created the universe. This theory of creation has been confirmed to a large extent by archaeological investigations carried out by Guy E. Pilgrim in 1915, who has established that 15 million years ago, early man lived in the Haryana Shivaliks. The Vamana Purana states that King Kuru ploughed the field of Kurukshetra with a golden ploughshare drawn by the Nandi of Lord Shiva and reclaimed an area of seven Kosas.Haryana has 6 administrative divisions, 22 districts, 72 sub-divisions, 93 revenue tehsils, 50 sub-tehsils, 140 community development blocks, 154 cities and towns, 6,841 villages and 6212 villages panchayats.The present book encompasses authoritative information on the past history, society, culture and economy. These topics are categorically discussed in modern context too.

Contents

1

State at a Glance

Haryana, carved out of the former state of East Punjab on 1 November 1966 on linguistic basis, is one of the 29 states in India. Situated in North India with less than 1.4% (44,212 km (17,070 sq mi)) of India's land area, it is ranked 21st in terms of area. Chandigarh is the capital, Faridabad in National Capital Region is the most populous city of the state and the Gurugramis the financial hub of NCR with major Fortune 500 companies located in it. Haryana has 6 administrative divisions, 22 districts, 72 sub-divisions, 93 revenue tehsils, 50 sub-tehsils, 140 community development blocks, 154 cities and towns, 6,841 villages and 6212 villages panchayats.

As the largest recipient of investment per capita since 2000 in India, and among one of the wealthiest and most economically developed regions in South Asia, Haryana has the sixth highest per capita income among Indian states and union territories at 180,174 (US$2,500) against the national average of 112,432 (US$1,600) for year 2016–17. Haryana's 2017-18 estimated state GSDP of US$95 billion (52% services, 30% industries and 18% agriculture) is growing at 12.96% 2012-17 CAGR and placed on the 14th position behind only much bigger states, is also boosted by 30 SEZs (mainly along DMIC, ADKIC and DWPE in NCR), 7% national agricultural exports, 60% of national Basmati rice export, 67% cars, 60% motorbikes, 50% tractors and 50% refrigerators produced in India. Faridabad has been described as eighth fastest growing city in the world and third most in India by City Mayors Foundation survey. In services, Gurugram ranks number 1 in India in IT growth rate and existing technology infrastructure, and number 2 in startup ecosystem, innovation and livability (Nov 2016).

Among the world's oldest and largest ancient civilizations, the Indus Valley Civilization sites at Rakhigarhi village in Hisar district and Bhirrana in Fatehabad district are 9,000 years old. Rich in history, monuments, heritage, flora and fauna, human resources and tourism with well developed economy, national highways and state roads, it is bordered by Himachal Pradesh to the north-east, by river Yamuna along its eastern border with Uttar Pradesh, by Rajasthan to the west and south, and Ghaggar-Hakra River flows along its northern border with Punjab. Since Haryana surrounds the country's capital Delhi on three sides (north, west and south), consequently a large area of Haryana is included in the economically-important National Capital Region for the purposes of planning and development.

ETYMOLOGY

The name Haryana is found in the works of the 12th-century AD Apabhramsha writer Vibudh Shridhar (VS 1189–1230). The name Haryana has been derived from the Sanskrit words *Hari* (the Hindu god Vishnu) and *ayana* (home), meaning "the Abode of God". However, scholars such as Muni Lal, Murli Chand Sharma, HA Phadke and Sukhdev Singh Chib believe that the name comes from a compound of the words *Hari* (Sanskrit *Harit*, "green") and *Aranya* (forest).

HISTORY

Pre-history

The Vedic state of Brahmavarta is claimed to be located in south Haryana, where the initial Vedic scriptures were composed after the great floods some 10,000 years ago. Rakhigarhi village in Hisar district and Bhirrana in Fatehabad district are home to the largest and one of the world's oldest ancient Indus Valley Civilization sites, dated at over 9,000 years old.

Evidence of paved roads, a drainage system, a large-scale rainwater collection storage system, terracotta brick and statue production, and skilled metal working (in both bronze and precious metals) have been uncovered. According to archaeologists, Rakhigarhi may be the origin of Harappan civilisation, which arose in the Ghaggar basin in Haryana and gradually and slowly moved to the Indus valley.

Medieval

Ancient bronze and stone idols of Jain Tirthankara were found in archaeological expeditions in Badli, Bhiwani (Ranila, Charkhi Dadri, Badhara village), Dadri, Gurgaon (Ferozpur Jhirka), Hansi, Hisar (Agroha), Kasan, Nahad, Narnaul, Pehowa, Rewari, Rohad, Rohtak (Asthal-Bohar) and Sonepat in Haryana.

After the sack of Bhatner fort during the Timurid conquests of India in 1398, Timur attacked and sacked the cities of Sirsa, Fatehabad, Sunam, Kaithal and Panipat. When he reached the town of Sarsuti, the residents, who were mostly non-Muslims, fled and were chased by a detachment of Timur's troops, with thousands of them being killed and looted by the troops. From there he travelled to Fatehabad, whose residents fled and a large number of those remaining in the town were massacred. The Ahirs resisted him at Ahruni but were defeated, with thousands being killed and many being taken prisoners while the town was burnt to ashes. From there he travelled to Tohana, whose Jat inhabitants were stated to be robbers according to Sharaf ad-Din Ali Yazdi. They tried to resist but were defeated and fled. Timur's army pursued and killed 200 Jats, while taking many more as prisoners. He then sent a detachment to chase the fleeing Jats and killed 2,000 of them while their wives and children were enslaved and their property plundered. Harveer Singh Gulia (1376 - 1398) was a Jat of the Gulia Clan from the village Badli; district Rohtak in Haryana, India. He was 22 years old when fought war with Timur. He was a strong and brave warrior. Timur proceeded to Kaithal whose residents were massacred and plundered, destroying all villages along the way. On the next day, he came to Assandh whose residents were "fire-worshippers" according to Yazdi, and had fled to Delhi. Next he travelled to and subdued Tughlaqpur fort and Salwan before reaching Panipat whose residents had already fled. He then marched on to Loni fort.Harveer Singh Gulia fought three fight with timur Battle of Delhi, Battle of Meerut, Battle of Haridwar.

Harveer Singh Gulia attacked Timur

The Deputy Commander Harveer Singh Gulia, along with 25,000 warriors of the Panchayat army, made a fierce attack on a big group of Timur's horsemen, and a fierce battle ensued where arrows and spears were used (There over 2, 000 hill archers joined the Panchayat Army. One arrow pierced Timur's hand. Timur was in the army of horsemen. Harveer Singh Gulia charged ahead like a lion, and hit Timur on his chest with a spear, and he was about to fall under his horse, when his commander Khijra, saved him and separated him from the horse.(Timur eventually died from this wound when he reached Samarkhand). The spearmen and swordsmen of the enemy leapt on the Harveer Singh Gulia, and he fainted from the wounds he received and fell. At that very time, the Supreme Commander Jograj Gujar, with 22,000 Mulls (warriors) attacked the enemy and killed 5000 horsemen. Jograj Gujjar himself with his own hands lifted the unconscious Harveer Singh Gulia and brought him to the camp. But a few hours later, the hero warrior Harveer Singh achieved martyrdom.

The area that is now Haryana has been ruled by some of the major empires of India. Panipat is known for three seminal battles in the history of India. In the First Battle of Panipat (1526), Babur defeated the Lodis. In the Second Battle of Panipat (1556), Akbar defeated the local Haryanvi Hindu Emperor of Delhi, who belonged to Rewari. Hem Chandra Vikramaditya had earlier won 22 battles across India from Punjab to Bengal, defeating Mughals and Afghans. Hemu had defeated Akbar's forces twice at Agra and the Battle of Delhi in 1556 to become the last Hindu Emperor of India with a formal coronation at Purana Quila in Delhi on 7 October 1556. In the Third Battle of Panipat (1761), the Afghan king Ahmad Shah Abdali defeated the Marathas.

Formation

Haryana as a state came into existence on 1 November 1966 the Punjab Reorganisation Act (1966). The Indian government set up the Shah Commission under the chairmanship of Justice JC Shah on 23 April 1966 to divide the existing state of Punjab and determine the boundaries of the new state of Haryana after consideration of the languages spoken by the people. The commission delivered its report on 31 May 1966 whereby the then-districts of Hisar, Mahendragarh, Gurgaon, Rohtak and Karnal were to be a part of the new state of Haryana. Further, the tehsils of Jind and Narwana in the Sangrur district — along with Naraingarh, Ambala and Jagadhri — were to be included.

The commission recommended that the tehsil of Kharad, which includes Chandigarh, the state capital of Punjab, should be a part of Haryana. However, only a small portion of Kharad was given to Haryana. The city of Chandigarh was made a union territory, serving as the capital of both Punjab and Haryana.Bhagwat Dayal Sharma became the first Chief Minister of Haryana.

HISTORICAL BACKGROUND

Haryana became a state of India on November 1, 1966. The present day Haryana is the region where, along the banks of the River Saraswati, the Vedic Civilization began and matured. It was here that the Vedas were written, as the Aryans chanted their sacred Mantras. Replete with myths and legends, Haryana's 5000 year old history is steeped in glory. It was here that Lord

Krishna preached Bhagvad Gita at the start of the battle of Mahabharata.

It was on this soil that saint Ved Vyas wrote Mahabharata in Sanskrit. Before the Mahabharata war, a battle of ten kings took place in the Kurukshetra region in the Saraswati valley. But it was the Mahabharata War, approximately in 900 BC, which gave to the region worldwide fame. Mahabharata knows Haryana as Bahudhhanyaka, land of plentiful grains and Bahudhana, the land of immense riches. The word Hariana, occurs in a 1328 AD Sanskrit inscription kept in the Delhi Museum, which refers to the Haryana region as The heaven on earth.

Excavations of various archeological sites in Haryana, like Naurangabad and Mittathal in Bhiwani, Kunal in Fatehabad, Agroha near Hissar, Rakhi Garhi (Rakhigarhi) in Jind, Sites in Rukhi (Rohtak) and Banawali in Sirsa have evidence of pre-Harappan and Harappan culture. Findings of pottery, sculpture and jewellery in sites at Pehowa, Kurukshetra, Tilpat and Panipat have proved the historicity of the Mahabharata war. These places are mentioned in the Mahabharata as Prithudaka (Pehowa), Tilprastha (Tilput), Panprastha (Panipat) and Sonprastha (Sonipat).

Haryana has been the scene of many wars because of it being "The Gateway of North India". As years rolled by, successive streams of Huns, Turks and the Afghans invaded India and decisive battles were fought on this land. After the downfall of the Gupta empire in the middle of 6th century AD north India was again split into several kingdoms. The Huns established their supremacy over the Punjab. It was after this period that one of the greatest King of ancient India, Harshvardhan began his rule. He became the King of Thanesar (Kurukshetra) in 606 AD, and later went on to rule the most of north India. In the 14th century, the Tomar kings led an army through this region to Delhi.

Later the Mughal, Babur, defeated the Lodhis in the first

battle of Panipat in the year 1526. Another decisive battle was fought in Panipat in 1556, establishing the reign of the Mughals for centuries to come. Taking advantage of Humayun's death, Hemu had marched to Agra and Delhi and occupied it without difficulty.

In response, Bairam Khan (Akbar's guardian) marched towards Delhi. Both the armies clashed in the second battle of Panipat. Hemu was in a winning position when a stray arrow struck him in the eye. He fell unconscious causing panic among his troops. The tide of the battle turned and the Mughals won the battle. Towards the middle of the 18th century, the Marathas had control over Haryana. The intrusion of Ahmed Shah Durrani in India, culminated in the third battle of Panipat in 1761. Marathas' defeat in this battle marked the end of their ascendancy and the decline of the Mughal Empire, leading to the advent of the British rule.

In 1857, the people of Haryana joined the Indian leaders in the 1857 Revolt against the British Government. By the end of June, 1857, most of the present Haryana region was liberated from the British. But the British managed to put down the rebellion in November, 1857 by bringing in additional forces from outside the area.

Indian history is replete with tales of heroism of the highest order and in this context, the historic significance of the battles of Panipat and Kurukshetra in Haryana cannot be ignored by any means. The sacrifices of Haryana's brave soldiers have played a very important role in maintaining the territorial and sovereign integrity of our nation. The new state which emerged as a separate political entity of the Indian Union on November 1, 1966, is considered to be the cradle of rich Indian cultural heritage. In terms of economic development too, Haryana has come a long way during the few past years.

Although Haryana is no longer a part of the state of Punjab, it was for a long time part of the Punjab province of British India and played a vital role in the history of the Punjab region.

ANCIENT CIVILIZATIONS

The ancient Saraswati River flowed through the northern part of present-day Haryana, and many consider the dry Ghaggar-Hakra River river bed to be that of the Saraswati. Many settlements dating back to the Indus Valley Civilization have been found along this river bed, at Naurangabad and Mittathal in Bhiwani District, Kunal in Fatehabad District, Agroha and Rakhigarhi in Hisar District, Rukhi in Rohtak District and Banawali in Sirsa District. The ancient Vedic civilization also flourished on the banks of the Saraswati, and the hymns of Rigveda were composed here.

In some ancient Hindu texts, the boundaries of Kurukshetra correspond roughly to the state of Haryana. Thus according to the Taittiriya Aranyaka 5.1.1., the Kurukshetra region is south of Turghna (Srughna/Sugh in Sirhind, Punjab), north of Khandava (Delhi and Mewat region), east of Maru (=desert) and west of Parin.

MAHABHARATA

The Epic Battle of Mahabharata at Kurukshetra.

Mahabharata, the great epic of India mentions Haryana as *Bahudhhanyaka*, 'land of plentiful grains' and *Bahudhana*, 'land of immense riches'. Several places mentioned in Mahabharata correspond to modern day cities in Haryana: Prithudaka (Pehowa), Tilprastha (Tilput), Panprastha (Panipat) and Sonprastha (Sonipat). Gurgaon refers to the village of the Guru Dronacharya .

The great battle between the Kauravas and the Pandavas took place near the city of Kurukshetra. Krishna preached the Bhagvad Gita to the reluctant Arjuna there. For eighteen days following that, armies from all over India battled in the plains of Kurukshetra to decide who sits on the throne of Hastinapur. Maharaja Agrasen is said to have established a flourishing city of merchants at Agroha near modern Hisar. Legend has it that anyone wishing to settle in the city was given a brick and a rupee by each of the city's lakh residents. Thus, they would have enough bricks to build a house and enough money to start a business of their own.

VEDIC CIVILIZATION

Vedic civilization is the earliest civilization in Indian history of which we have written records that we understand. It is named after the Vedas, the early literature of the Hindu people. The Vedic Civilization flourished along the river Saraswati, in a region that now consists of the modern Indian states of Haryana and Punjab. The Vedic texts have astronomical dates, that some have claimed, go back to the 5th millennium BC. The use of Vedic Sanskrit continued up to the 6th century BC. Vedic is synonymous with Aryans and Hinduism, which is another name for religious and spiritual thought that has evolved from the Vedas.

The Early Aryans: Unfortunately, the origin of the Saraswati Valley civilization (Vedic culture) and its relation to the Indus Valley civilization remain hazy. The timeline of Vedic civilization is 4500 BC-1800 BC while that of Indus valley civilization is 3300 BC-1800 BC. The texts describe geography that some believe to be north India. The greatest river of the Rigveda was Saraswati, now dry and identified with Ghaggar, a seasonal river.

It is believed that this river ceased to reach the Arabian Sea by about 1900 BC. Now, a dry river bed, that seems to fit the description of the Saraswati River, has been detected by satellite imagery. It begins in the modern Indian state of Uttaranchal and passing through Haryana, Punjab, and Rajasthan, reaches the Arabian Sea in Gujarat. Our knowledge of the early Aryans comes from the Rigveda, the earliest of the Vedas.

Political Organization: The grama (village), vis and jana were political units of the early Aryans. A vis was probably a subdivision of a jana and a grama was probably a smaller unit than the other two. The leader of a grama was called gramani and that of a vis was called vispati. Another unit was the gana whose head was a jyeshta (elder). The rashtra (state) was governed by a rajan (king). The king is often referred to as gopa (protector) and samrat (supreme ruler). He governed the people with their consent and approval.

It is possible that he was sometimes elected. The sabha and samiti were popular councils. The main duty of the king was to protect the tribe. He was aided by two functionaries, the purohita (chaplain) and the senani (army chief; sena: army). The former not only gave advice to the ruler but also practiced spells and charms for success in war. Soldiers on foot (patti) and on chariots (rathins), armed with bow and arrow were common. The king employed spasa (spies) and dutas (messengers). He often got a ceremonial gift, bali, from the people.

Society and Economy: Rig Vedic society was characterized by a nomadic lifestyle with cattle rearing being the chief occupation. The Aryans kept hordes of cattle and cows were held in high esteem. Milk was an important part of the diet. Agriculture was equally important and went hand in hand with cattle rearing.

It grew more prominent with time as the community settled down. The cow was also the standard unit of barter; coins were not used in this period. Families were patrilineal, and people prayed for abundance of sons. Education of women was not neglected, and some even composed Rig Vedic hymns. Marriage for love as well as for money was known. The concept of caste and hereditary nature of profession was unknown to the early Aryans.

The food of the early Aryans consisted of parched grain and cakes, milk and milk products, and fruits and vegetables. Consumption of meat was common. A passage in the Rig Veda describes how to apportion the meat of a sacrificed horse. It must be borne in mind that vegetarianism took firm root in India only after the rise of Buddhism in the sixth century BC.

MAHABHARATHA WAR

Mahabharata, (or Mahabharata as it is known in English), is the longest poem in the world, made up of 220, 000 lines divided into 18 sections. It was written in Sanskrit, the ancient sacred language of India and it tells the story of a great battle that occurred about 3000 years back. It was on the banks of river Saraswati that saint Ved Vyas wrote Mahabharata, approximately in 900 BC. Lord Krishna preached 'Bhagvad Gita', the gospel of duty, to Arjun at the on set of the great battle of Mahabharata. Since then, this profound philosophy of the supremacy of duty has became the foundation of Hinduism, Indian culture and thought. The Mahabharata knows Haryana as "Bahudhhanyaka" - The land of plentiful grains, and "Bahudhana" - The land of immense riches.

Dhritarashter and Pandu were born to Bhisham's brothers. Dhritarashter was born blind and though the elder, he had to forfeit his claim to the throne due to this physical defect. Pandu became king. Of the two brothers Dhritarashter married Gandhari, whereas Pandu, the younger had two wives, Kunti and Madri. Gandhari was so devoted to her husband that she bandaged her eyes, not to enjoy anything that she could not share with her royal husband, and thus remained voluntarily blind for life. She became the mother of the Kouravs, 100 in total, whereas Kunti got three sons and Madri two.

One day while hunting, Pandu accidentally killed the wife of a sage, who got enraged and cursed Pandu that if ever he had intercourse with a woman, he would die instantly. Pandu renounced his crown to become a hermit and went to the jungle with his two wives, Kunti and Madri.

But one day, Pandu couldn't resist himself and had intercourse with Madri and thus died. Madri immolated herself and walked into her husband's funeral fire leaving behind her two sons Nakul and Sahadev in custody of Kunti who already had three sons Yudhisthira, Bheem and Arjuna. On Pandu's death Dhritarashter became the king and the five sons of

Pandu, known as the Pandavs grew up in the guardianship of Kunti.

The five Pandav princes were educated along with Kourav boys under the supervision of Bhisham and the patronage of Dhritarashter. Drone, though a Brahmin was a very skilful and efficient teacher, who taught them the art of archery and the various techniques of warfare.

Yudhisthira, the eldest of the Pandavs, was so righteous that he gained the name Dharamputr. Bheem was a giant in physical strength. Arjuna was handsome and the most skilful archer. Dharamputr was the beloved of the people and being the eldest among the 105 princes, was naturally, and by his right too, the heir to the throne. Duryodhan, the eldest of the Kouravs, however was jealous of the Pandavs and tried every means to destroy them.

When Yudhisthira was proclaimed king, Duryodhan could not sit quiet and watch. Dhritarashter loved all the 105 princes alike, and there was no partiality in his mind between his own sons and the nephews, the Pandavs. The great blind royal father, came under the bad influence of Duryodhan and, though directly not an evil-doer, was in sympathy with his son's disappointments and sorrows.

Duryodhan's plan to kill the Pandavs cunningly giving poison to Bheem, burning down the lac-house etc., failed miserably. Bheem was strong enough to digest the poison. The Pandavs were warned in time by their uncle Vidur and so in the darkness of the night the five brothers along with their mother escaped into the jungle from the burning lac-house. After their miraculous escape from the lac-house, they did not return to the palace. They roamed about in the guise of Brahmins with their mother. Every one including the Kouravs believed them to be dead.

During that time, they heard of the Swayamvara of Droupadi. The qualification to marry her lay in the extraordinary skill of archery in hitting a moving target. Arjuna easily won.

Everybody congratulated the winner, and discovered that it was Arjuna.

Thus the Pandavs were found out, He took his bride to their hut and called to his mother to come outside and see what he had brought. Instead of doing so, she answered back "My dear children, whatever it be, you share it among yourselves". Therefore, Droupadi became the common wife of all the five Pandavs. Krishna, who was also present, at the marriage ceremony became a great friend of the Pandavs from then onwards. On Bhisham's advice, the kingdom was divided into two parts.

Naturally the better half was taken away by the Kouravs. Still, the others built a wonderful city in their own half and called it Indraprastha. Duryodhan watching the increasing prosperity of the Pandavs and could contain himself no longer. He openly challenged Dharamputr for a game of dice, Sakuni, deceit in human form, was the uncle of the Kouravs. He played for them. Inevitably Dharamputr lost everything - his kingdom, his brothers and also his wife.

Not satisfied with this gain, Duryodhan tried to insult Droupadi in public. By Lord Krishna's grace, nothing disastrous happened. Dhritarashter, fearing that this might bring unforeseen calamities begged Droupadi to take whatever she wanted. She asked for the freedom of her husbands.

It was granted. Dhritarashter due to his excessive love for the eldest son was blind to what is right and what is wrong. So again Duryodhan invited Dharamputr for another game of dice, and the bet was that the losers would live in the forest for 13 years without any claim to the kingdom, the last year however to be spent incognito. But if in the thirteenth year, they were detected, again a round of 13 years' exile; and this would go on forever.

Dharamputr lost again. During the twelve years in the forests, the Pandavs visited many holy places. They had many interesting adventures at this time. One of them led to Hanuman's friendship and grace. Arjuna is called Kapidhvaja as he keeps on his flag the emblem of Hanuman. Krishna visited them now and then. Arjuna, at the advice of Vyasa, practiced penance, propitiated Shiva and got from Him the mighty weapon, the Pasupatastra. He propitiated also the other gods lndra, Agni, Varuna and others and got from all of them very powerful weapons. Thus the twelve years were not wasted but spent in securing the divine weapons, which would become useful later on.

In the 13th year, hiding all their weapons in the hollow of a tree in a burial ground, all the Pandavs with Droupadi went to the palace of the king of the Viratas and stayed there as servants. Duryodhan was making frantic efforts to discover them. When he heard about the strange murder of Kichaka the brother-in-law of the king, he concluded that the Pandavs must be in the Virata country. So the Kouravs attacked the Viratas, with apparent purpose of carrying away its cattle-wealth. Of course the Pandavs took part in the battle, but when they were recognized as Pandavs the time limit of thirteen years had already passed.

Dharamputr was fond of peace, and was ever against any quarrel, much less war. So he sent Krishna as a messenger to Hastinapur to claim his kingdom back from Duryodhan. But Duryodhan had by this time come to regard Indraprastha as his own. He not only refused to give their kingdom back, but refused to give even 5 houses for the five brothers to live! War had to be declared. This is the great war fought at Kurukshetra to decide the right of claim.

The hundred Kouravs, Bhisham, Drone, Asvathama, etc., were on one side and the Pandavs, Krishna, Drupada, etc., were on the other. Krishna did not actually fight. He was the charioteer of Arjuna and hence He is called Parthasarathy. Krishna was very impartial. He gave his army to the Kouravs and himself offered to serve the Pandavs. The Kourav and the Pandav armies arrayed themselves for the war.

The Kouravs planned their attacks under the supervision of Bhisham, and under Bheem's management the Pandava army marched into formation. This is the point at which Arjuna has second thoughts about fighting in the battle. Krishna gives Arjuna good advise that brings back his war-spirit. This advice is known as: The Bhagvad-Gita.

All the Kourav princes died in this battle, and Yudhisthira became king. He continued to reign until he felt that he had completed his life's work. Then he renounced the throne and set out for heaven with the other Pandavs and their wife, Droupadi. With them also went a dog which represented Dharma, the god of duty and moral law. After more adventures, the Pandavs were finally united in heaven.

This story, which forms the main theme of the Mahabharata, makes up only about a quarter of the poem. The Mahabharata contains many other popular stories, including the tales of Nala and Damayanti, Savitri and Satyawan, Rama, and Shakuntala.

The battle of Kurukshetra offers an opportunity to discuss military strategy, there is also a mention of a board game *Chaturanga*, from which the modern day Chess originated. But the underlying theme of the Mahabharata concerns moral duty and right conduct. The long and complex dispute that divides the royal family of Bharat affords an opportunity to explain the duties and conduct expected of a king. It also shows the ideals of behaviour for subjects, soldiers, religious hermits, and people suffering misfortune.

Sage Ved Vyasa is traditionally regarded as the author of the Mahabharata, but he is more likely to have been its compiler. The epic seems to be a collection of writings by several authors who lived at various times. The oldest parts are probably about 3, 000 years old, while others can be traced to as late as AD 500. The importance of Krishna as the main god of this epic developed in Hindu thought between 200 BC and AD 200.

As a result, the Mahabharata can be used to trace the spread and development of Vaishnavite thought in Hinduism. The god

Vishnu became a very personal deity for his worshippers through his appearance as Krishna, the adviser and friend of Prince Arjuna in the Mahabharata. About 1, 300 greatly varying manuscripts of the Mahabharata survive today. All of them show the poem in its later form because the earliest of them goes back only to the 1400's.

The most famous addition to the Mahabharata is the Bhagvad-Gita. It occurs in the sixth book and is now the most widely recognized of Hinduism's sacred texts. The Bhagvad Gita tells how Arjuna, the third of the Pandav princes, has misgivings about whether he should be fighting his cousins, the Kouravs. Krishna, speaking with the authority of the god Vishnu, persuades him that his action is just, and then Arjuna's military skill becomes a deciding factor in the ensuing Pandav victory. The teachings of the Bhagvad-Gita are fundamental to Hinduism.

KING HARSHVARDHAN

Harshvardhan (606-647 AD)

After the downfall of the Gupta Empire in the middle of the sixth century AD, North India was again split into several independent kingdoms. The Huns established their supremacy over the Punjab and certain other parts of Central India. The northern and western regions of India passed into the hands of a dozen or more feudatories. Gradually, one of them, Prabhakar Vardhana, the ruler of Thanesar, who belonged to the Pushabhukti family, extended his control over all other feudatories.

Prabhakar Vardhan was the first king of the Vardhan dynasty with his capital at Thanesar now a small town in the vicinity of Kurukshetra in the state of Haryana nearly 150 km. from Delhi. After his death in A.D. 606, his eldest son, RajyaVardhan, ascended the throne. He was killed in a battle which he won against Devagupta who had killed Grahavarman, the husband of his sister Rajyashri and usurped the throne of Kannauj.

Harsha ascended the throne at the age of 16. Though quite a young man, he proved himself a great conqueror and an able administrator. After his accession, Harsha first rescued his sister just as she was going to commit Sati. At the request of his sister, he united the two kingdoms of Thanesar (Kurukshetra) and Kannauj and transferred his capital from Thanesar to Kannauj. Harsha waged many wars he defeated Sasank of Bengal. He also brought the five Indies i.e. Eastern Punjab (present day Haryana, Kannauj, Bengal, Bihar and Orissa under his control. He conquered Dhruvasena of Gujarat. He also conquered Ganjam, a part of the modern Orissa State.

His empire included territories of distant feudal kings too. Harsha governed his empire on the same lines a the Guptas. The kings he conquered paid him revenue and sent soldiers when he was fighting war. They accepted his sovereignty, but remained rulers over their own kingdoms. Harsha's ambition of extending his power to the Deccan and southern India were stopped by Pulakesin II, the Chalukya king of Vatapi in northern Mysore.

His reign is comparatively well-documented, thanks to his court poet Bana and Hieun Tsang. Bana composed an account of Harsha's rise to power in 'Harshacharita'. Hieun Tsang was a Chinese Buddhist pilgrim who came to India during this time to collect Buddhist literature and to visit places connected with Buddhism. He wrote a full description of his journey in his book 'SI-YU-KI'. Harsha died in the year 647 AD. He ruled over India for 41 years. He was the last empire builder of ancient India. Harsha supported the development of philosophy and literature and wrote three well-known plays - Nagananda, Ratnavali and Priyadarsika.

After Harsha's death, apparently without any heirs, his empire died with him. The kingdom disintegrated rapidly into small states. The succeeding period is very obscure and badly documented, but it marks the culmination of a process which had begun with the invasion of the Hunas in the last years of the Gupta Empire. Meanwhile, the kingdoms of the Deccan and the south became powerful.

MEDIEVAL PERIOD

After ousting the Huns, king Harshvardhan established his capital at Thanesar near Kurukshetra in the 7th century AD. After his death, the kingdom disintegrated. The region, however, remained strategically important for the rulers of Delhi, as it lay in the path of invaders from the northwest. Prithviraj Chauhan established a fort at Hansi in the 12th century.

Muhammad Ghori conquered this area in the Second Battle of Tarain. Following his death, the Delhi Sultanate was established that ruled much of India for several centuries.

The earliest reference to 'Hariana' occurs in a Sanskrit inscription dated 1328 AD kept in Delhi Museum which refers to this region as *The heaven on earth*, indicating that it was fertile and relatively peaceful at that time. Firoz Shah Tughluq established a fort at Hisar in 1354 to further fortify the region.

The three famous battles of Panipat took place near the modern town of Panipat.

The first battle took place in 1526, where Babur, the ruler of Kabul defeated Ibrahim Lodhi of the Delhi Sultanate, through the use of field artillery.

This battle marked the beginning of the Mughal Empire in India. In the second battle of Panipat (November 5, 1556), Akbar's general Bairam Khan defeated Hemu, and paved the way for Akbar's reign. The third battle of Panipat marked the end of the Maratha Empire in India. On January 13, 1761, the Maratha forces were decisively defeated by the Afghan forces led by Ahmed Shah Abdali.

BATTLE OF PANIPAT

The 1526 Battle of Panipat and the death of Sultan Ibrahim,

the last of the Lodi sultans of Delhi. However, while the Timurids were united, the Lodi armies were far from unified. Ibrahim was widely detested, even amongst his nobles, and it was several of his Afghan nobles who were to invite Babar's intervention. Babar assembled a 12,000-man army, and advanced into India. This number actually increased as Babar advanced, as members of the local population joined the invading army. The first major clash between the two sides was fought in late February 1526. Babar's son, Humayun (then aged 17), led the Timurid army into battle against the first of Ibrahim's advance parties. Humayun's victory was harder fought than the previous skirmishes, but it was still a decisive victory. Over one hundred prisoners of war were captured along with around eight war elephants. However, unlike after previous battles, these prisoners were not bonded or freed; by decree from Humayun, they were shot. In his memoirs, Babar recorded that "Ustad Ali-quli and the matchlockmen were ordered to shoot all the prisoners, by way of example; this had been Humayun's first affair, his first experience of battle; it was an excellent omen!" This is perhaps the earliest example of execution by firing squad.

Ibrahim Lodi advanced against him with 100,000 soldiers and 100 elephants; and though Babar's army had grown, it was still less than half the size of his opponents, possibly as few as 25,000 men. This was to be their main engagement, the First battle of Panipat, and was fought on 21 April 1526. Ibrahim Lodi was slain and his army was routed; Babar quickly took possession of both Delhi and Agra. That very day Babar ordered Humayun to ride to Agra (Ibrahim's former capital) and secure its national treasures and resources from looting. Humayun found the family of the Raja of Gwalior there — the Raja himself having died at Panipat — sheltering from the invaders, fearing the dreadful nature of the 'Mongols' from the stories that preceded their arrival. After their safety was guaranteed they gave Humayun their family's most valuable jewel, a very large diamond, which some believe to be the diamond which came to be called the Koh-i-Noor or "Mountain of Light'. It is thought that they did this to retain their Kingdom. Whether it was because of the gift or not, the family remained the rulers of Gwalior, though now under their new rulers the Timurids.

Babar, meanwhile, marched onward to Delhi reaching it three days after the battle. He celebrated his arrival with a festival on the river Jumna, and remained there at least until Friday prayers (Jum'ah) at noon when he heard the Khutba (sermon), read in his name in the Jama Masjid, a sign of the recognition of his sovereignty. He then marched to Agra to join Humayun. Upon arrival Babar was presented with the fabulous diamond, and Babar reports that "I just gave it back to him", adding, "an expert in jewels said its value would provide two and a half days food for the whole world."

Battles with the Rajputs

Khusrau Shah Kokultash pays homage and fealty to Babar, prior to the Battle of Khanwa. Although master of Delhi and Agra, Babar records in his memoirs that he had sleepless nights because of continuing worries over Raja Hasan Khan, Mewatpatti (title, Lord of Mewat), the Khanzada ruler of Mewat, Rana Sanga, the Rajput ruler of Mewar.

In A.D. 1526 a new power appeared in India. Babar, who claimed to be the representative of Timur Lang, after winning the battle of Panipat, took possession of Delhi and Agra ; and determined that his enterprise should not be a mere raid like Timur's, but the foundation of a new and lasting empire. Then it was that the Rajputs made their last great struggle for independence. They were led by Rana Sanga, a chief of Mewar, who invited the Mewatti chief, Hasan Khan, to aid the nation from which he had sprung in resisting the new horde of Musalmans from the north.

The political position of Hasan Khan at this time was a very important one. Babar, in his autobiography, speaks of him as the prime mover in all the confusions and insurrections of the period.

He had, he states, vainly shown Hasan Khan distinguished marks of favour, but the affections of the infidel lay all on the side of the natives i.e., the Hindus (Indians); and the propinquity of his country to Delhi, no doubt, made his opposition especially dangerous. Hasan Khan's seat at this time was at Ulwur, but local tradition says that he was originally established at Bahadarpur, eight miles from Ulwur.

Babar says that the ancestors of his opponent Hasan Khan had governed Mewat in uninterrupted succession for nearly 200 years, and that Tejara was their capital. In another place he calls him Raja Hasan Khan Mewati, an infidel, who was the prime mover and agitator in the insurrection against the Mughals. The title of Raja and the term " infidel " show that Babar was aware of Hasan Khan's Hindu descent, and the period of '* nearly 200 years" most probably refers to the date when his ancestor became a Muslim in the reign of Firoz Shah between A.H. 752 and 790.The Rajput lords had, prior to Babar's intervention, succeeded in conquering some of the Sultanate's territory. They ruled an area directly to the southwest of Babar's new dominions, commonly known as Rajputana as well as fortified dominions in other parts of northern India. It was not a unified kingdom, but rather a coalition of principalities, under the informal suzerainty of Rana Sanga, head of the senior Rajput dynasty. The Rajputs had possibly heard word of the heavy casualties caused by Lodi on Babar's forces, and believed that they could capture Delhi, and possibly all Hindustan. They hoped to bring it back into Hindu Rajput hands for the first time in almost three hundred and fifty years since Sultan Shah-al Din Muhammad of Ghor defeated the Rajput Chauhan King Prithviraj III in 1192.

Furthermore, the Rajputs were well aware that there was dissent within the ranks of Babar's army. The hot Indian summer was upon them, and many troops wanted to return home to the cooler climes of Central Asia. The Rajputs' position for courage preceded them, and their superior numbers no doubt further contributed to the desire of Babar's army to retreat. According to Babar's own calculations the potential strength of the Rajput army was much larger than that deployed by the Lodis at Panipat. Babar resolved to make this an extended battle, and decided to push further into India, into lands never previously claimed by the Timurids. He needed his troops to defeat the Rajputs. Despite the unwillingness of his troops to engage in further warfare, Babar was convinced he could overcome the Rajputs and gain complete control over Hindustan. He made great propaganda of the fact that for the first time he was to battle non-Muslims, the Kafir, to the extent of taking a vow to abstain from drinking (a common fraction among his people) for the rest of his life to win divine favour, and declared the war against Rana Sanga.

After Babar fell seriously ill, Humayun was told of a plot by the senior nobles of Babar's court to bypass the leader's sons and appoint Mahdi Khwaja, Babar's sister's husband, as his successor. He rushed to Agra and arrived there to see his father was well enough again, although Mahdi Khwaja had lost all hope of becoming ruler after arrogantly exceeding his authority during Babar's illness. Upon his arrival in Agra it was Humayun himself who fell ill, and was close to dying.

Babar died at the age of 47 on January 5 [O.S. 26 December 1530] 1531, and was succeeded by his eldest son, Humayun. Though he wished to be buried in his favourite garden in Kabul, a city he had always loved, he was first buried in a mausoleum in the capital city of Agra. His remains were later moved to Bagh-e Babar (Babar Gardens) in Kabul, Afghanistan. The Persian inscription on his tomb there translates as "If there is a paradise on earth, it is this, it is this, it is this! Unlike in India, Babar is considered a national hero in Uzbekistan and Kyrgyzstan, and is held in high esteem in Afghanistan. In October 2005 Pakistan developed the Babar (cruise missile), named in his honour.

F. Lehmann has said that, His origin, milieu, training, and culture were steeped in Persian culture and so Babar was largely responsible for the fostering of this culture by his descendants, the Mughals of India, and for the expansion of Persian cultural influence in the Indian subcontinent, with brilliant literary, artistic, and historiographical results.

Babar is popularly believed to have demolished the Rama Temple at Ayodhya and built Babri Mosque in Ayodhya. However, from the three inscriptions which once decorated the surface of the mosque it becomes apparent that the mosque was constructed during his reign on the orders of Mir Baqi, who was one of the generals of Babar's forces sent towards this region.

FIRST BATTLE OF PANIPAT (1526 AD)

The first Battle of Panipat gave a death blow to the Lodhi Empire and marked the end of the Delhi Sultanate's rule in India. It led to the establishment of the Mughal Empire in India. Mongol prince Zahir-ud-Din Muhammad, known as Babur, had promised to help Daulat Khan Lodhi, Governor of Lahore, to fight the Sultan of Delhi Ibrahim Lodhi in 1523 and made many raids into Punjab. Babur, after occupying the whole of Panjab by 1525 AD, marched towards Delhi.

In November 1525 he set out to meet the Sultan of Delhi. Passage of Indus took place on 15th December. Babur had about 12, 000 soldiers. Crossing Sutluj at Roper and reached Ambala without meeting any resistance. On April 1st Babur reached Panipat. It was barren wasteland dry and naked with few thorny bushes. Rumors came that Sultan was coming with an army of 100, 000 and 1000 war elephants. The Afghan Sultan of Delhi, Ibrahim Lodhi advanced from Delhi to meet the invader. Babur had a strong artillery which was effectively pressed into service.

The battle started at six in the morning. Sultan Ibrahim Lodhi advanced rapidly. At about 400 yards Babur's Cannons opened fire, noise and smoke from the artillery terrified the Afghans and the attack lost momentum. Seizing the movement Babur sent out his flanking columns to envelop the Sultan's army. Here the Afghans met for the first time the real weapon of Mongols 'Turko-Mongol Bow'.

Its superiority lay in the fact that it was the weapon of the nobles, of the finest warriors. Such a bow in the hands of a Mongol warrior would shoot three times as rapidly as musket and could kill at 200 yards.

Attacked from 3 sides the Afghans jammed into each other. Elephants hearing noise of cannon at close range ran wildly out of control. Ibrahim Lodhi and about 6000 of his troops were involved in actual fighting. Most of his army stretching behind up to a mile never saw action. Battle ended in about 3 hours with the death of Ibrahim Lodhi who was at forefront.

And in place where fighting had been the fiercest, among the heap of Mongols slain of his sword, lay the vain but courageous Sultan Ibrahim Lodhi.

His head was cut off and taken to Babur. Ibrahim Lodhi's tomb is still present in Panipat. When Afghans fled they left 20, 000 dead and wounded. Losses to Babur's army were heavy 4000 of his troops were killed or wounded. Had Sultan Ibrahim survived another hour of fighting he would have won, as Babur had no reserves and his troops were rapidly tiring in Indian midday sun.

Babur observes in his autobiography, "The mighty army of Delhi was laid in the dust in the course of half a day." In the words of Rushbrook Williams, "If there was one single material factor, which more than any other conduced to his ultimate triumph in Hindustan, it was his powerful artillery." The elephants trampled their own soldiers after being frightened away by the explosion of gunpowder.

Two weeks later the victorious Babur entered Agra where he was presented with the famous diamond 'Koh-i-noor'. Babur celebrated his victory in a lavish manner and occupied Delhi and Agra.

SECOND BATTLE OF PANIPAT (1556 AD)

On 24th January, 1556 AD Mughal ruler Humayun slipped while climbing down the steps of his library and fell to his death. His son Akbar was only thirteen years old when he ascended the throne. At the time of Akbar's accession to the throne, the Mughal rule was confined to Kabul, Kandhahar, and parts of Punjab and Delhi. Akbar was then campaigning in Punjab with his chief minister Bairam Khan.

On February 14, 1556, in a garden at Kalanaur, Akbar was enthroned as emperor. Hemu (Hemchandra) was a military chief of the Afghan King Muhammad Adil Shah who had established himself at Chunar and was seeking to expel the Mughals from India. Taking advantage of Humayun's death, Hemu marched to Agra and Delhi in October and occupied it without difficulty, and became the ruler under the title 'Raja Vikramaditya'.

To counter this, Bairam Khan (Akbar's guardian) marched towards Delhi. On November 5 both the armies met at Panipat. Hemu with a large army including 1, 500 war elephants had initial success. There was a pitched battle and Hemu was on a winning spree when a stray arrow struck him in the eye. He fell unconscious. As in many other battles, the loss of the leader caused panic among the troops and turned the tide of the battle.

The Mughals won the battle. Shah Quli Khan captured the Hawai elephant with its prize occupant, and took it directly to Akbar. Hemu was brought unconscious before Bairam and Akbar. Bairam pleaded Akbar to perform the holy duty of slaying the infidel and earn the Islamic holy title of 'Ghazi'. Among much self-congratulation Akbar then severed the head of unconscious Hemu with his saber.

Some historians claim that Akbar did not kill Hemu himself, but just touched the infidel's head with his sword and his associates finished the gory 'holy' work. After the battle Hemu's head was sent to Kabul as a sign of victory to the ladies of Humayun's harem, and Hemu's torso was sent to Delhi for exposure on a gibbet.

Iskandar Khan chased the Hemu's fleeing army and captured 1500 elephants and a large contingent. Hemu's wife escaped from Delhi with the treasure and Pir Muhammad Khan's troops chased her caravan without success.

There was a great slaughter of those who were captured and in keeping with the custom of his ancestors. Akbar had a victory pillar built with their heads. This battle, known as Second Battle of Panipat was an epoch-making event in the history of India as it resulted in re-establishment of the Mughal Empire in India.

BRITISH RULE

During the British rule, most of Haryana formed part of the Punjab province. Some parts were ruled by the princely states of Nabha, Jind and Patiala. During the Indian rebellion of 1857, several leaders from this region, including Rao Tula Ram, participated actively. Later, leaders like Sir Chhotu Ram played an important role in the politics of the Punjab province.

BATTLE OF KARNAL 1739 AD

February 24, 1739, battle between the forces of Nadir Shah, an Iranian adventurer, and Muhammad Shah, the Mughal emperor, at Karnal, 125 km north of Delhi; the Mughals suffered a decisive defeat. Nadir led about 55, 000 troops, and Muhammad 15, 000, but both sides, especially the Indian, had large numbers of noncombatants. Nadir Shah had become the ruler of Persia by deposing the King in 1732.

Nadir began his invasion in 1738 AD by pursuing fugitives from Kandhahar to Mughal-held Kabul (both now in Afghanistan). The alleged violation of promises by Muhammad Shah, and the ill-treatment of his envoys by the Delhi court, served as the alleged cause for his invasion. Divided counsels prevented a Mughal stand until Nadir reached Karnal. Jealousy and rashness led to the Indian defeat, and the emperor was besieged in his entrenched camp. Nadir marched to Delhi and massacred its inhabitants on March 11. He left Delhi on May 5 with plunder, including the famous Peacock Throne of Shah Jahan and the Kohinoor diamond. The Mughal Empire never recovered from this blow to its prestige.

THIRD BATTLE OF PANIPAT (1761)

Towards the middle of the 18th century, Marathas, under the leadership of the Peshwas had established their sway over Haryana and most of North India. The intrusion of the Afghan, Ahmed Shah Abdali into India, culminated in the third battle of Panipat on January 14, 1761. Ahmad Shah defeated the Marathas and this marked the end of the Maratha ascendancy. The defeat of the Marathas, rapid decline of the Mughal Empire after Aurangzeb's death, leading ultimately to the advent of the British rule.

The main reasons for the failure of Marathas were the lack of allies. Though their infantry was based on European style contingent, they failed to woo allies in North India. Their earlier behaviour and their political ambitions which led them to loot and plunder had antagonized all the powers. They had interfered in the internal affairs of the Rajputana states (present day Rajasthan) and levied heavy taxes and huge fines on them.

They had also made huge territorial and monetary claims upon Awadh. Their raids in the Sikh territory had angered the Sikh chiefs. Similarly the Jat chiefs, on whom also they had imposed heavy fines, did not trust them. They had, therefore, to fight their enemies alone, except for the weak support of Imad -ul-Mulk. Moreover, the senior Maratha chiefs constantly bickered with one another. Each one of them had ambitions of carving out their independent states and had no interest in fighting against a common enemy.

Ahmad Shah (1722-73), first emir of Afghanistan, was the hereditary chief of the Abdali tribe of Afghans, whom he later renamed the Durrani. He led a contingent of his tribesmen in the service of Nadir Shah, king of Persia, who won control of most of Afghanistan and part of India. When Nadir died, Ahmad founded an independent Afghan kingdom. He invaded the Indian Punjab six times between 1748 and 1752, and he seized and sacked Delhi. Although he was a powerful military leader, Ahmad never succeeded in permanently ruling India; he subsequently withdrew into Afghanistan.

HISTORY FROM 1803 TO 1857

The year 1803 is an important year in the history of Haryana. In this year the area of what is now present day Haryana and Delhi came under the control of the East India Company of Great Britain. At that time Delhi was being ruled by the old and week Mughal ruler Shah Alam. But the real power lay in the hands of the Maratha leader Daulat Rao Sindhiya, who acted as his Regent.

On 6th September, 1803 the battle between General Lake's British forces and the Marathas took place near village Partapganj, 6 miles south of Delhi. Many people from Haryana fought along with the Marathas against the British. Among them were the Jats, led by Hari Singh, the king of Ballabhgarh, Ahirs, led by Rao Tej Singh of Rewari and 5000 Sikhs.

The Marathas fought bravely but lost due to the cowardice of French officers who were assisting them. When the British entered Delhi on 14 September, 1803, the Mughal ruler Shah Alam surrendered. On 30 September, 1803, the Maratha leader Daulat Rao Sindhiya also decided to make peace with the British by signing a treaty with the East India Company. Under this treaty the areas of Haryana and Delhi came under the control of the British.

In 1805 the British divided this area into 2 parts for administrative and political reasons. A smaller part called the 'Assigned Territories' was kept directly under the control of the Company. The larger part was divided and handed over to various local ruler who were faithful and loyal to the British.

The Assigned Territory consisted of the areas under Panipat, Sonipat, Samalkha, Ganaur, Palam, Palwal, Nuh, Nagina, Hathin, Ferozepur Jhirkha, Sohna and Rewari. This area was administered by East India Company officer called the 'Resident' and he reported directly to the Governor General. The other larger part was divided into various princely states and handed over to loyal local kings and nawabs.

But these arrangements didn't go down too well with the people of Haryana, who are by nature independent minded and dont like outsiders meddling in their affairs. Therefore they, especially the Jats of Rohtak and Ahirs & Meos of Gurgaon, rose again and again in revolt against the rulers. But by 1809 the British had established full control over the territory of Haryana.

Year 1833 was another important landmark in Haryana's history. In this year the Bengal Presidency under the East India Company, was divided into two provinces of Bengal and North Western Province. Most areas of Haryana and Delhi together became one of the six divisions of the North Western Province called the Delhi division. The Delhi division was further sub-divided into seven princely states and five districts.

The princely states were Bahadurgarh, Ballabhgarh, Dujana, Farukhnagar, Jhajjar, Loharu and Pataudi. The five districts were Delhi, Gurgaon, Rohtak, Panipat and Hissar. These districts were divided into Tehsils and Tehsils into 'Zails'. The officer heading the Delhi division was now called a Commissioner instead of the 'Resident'. At this time some areas of present day Haryana were outside the Delhi division and they were considered as part of the 'upper region'. These were the districts of Ambala and Thanesar and the princely states of Buria, Chhachhrauli and Jind. But the people of 'upper region' and Delhi division though administratively in different provinces, were closely bound by sociocultural ties. This administrative system continued till the revolt of 1857.

The revolt of 1857 was sparked by the introduction of the

Enfield rifle in the Indian Army. The cartridges of this new rifle were greased with an ingredient containing 'cow's fat' and 'hog's lard'. This news spread like wild fire among the sepoys of the army. Both Hindus and the Muslims were shocked and outraged at the use of 'cow's fat' and 'hog's lard' respectively. They soon formed panchayats in all corps and decided to socially boycott any sepoy who used these cartridges.

This feeling continued to grow until at last a spirit of mutiny spread throughout northern India and Bengal. The first military station in northern India where the mutiny started was Ambala on 10 May, 1857. Except for the princely states of Jind, Kalsia, Buria and some small Jagirs in Ambala and Thanesar, whole of the Haryana region was severely affected by the revolt. An important aspect of the uprising in Haryana was complete communal cooperation and amity. By the start of June, 1857 almost whole of Haryana had become independent of the British rule.

It took almost six months for the British to take back the control of Haryana. This they managed by the use of superior firearms, artillery and the help of some loyal rulers of princely states. The rebels were ruthlessly crushed by the British and in doing so they burned down hundreds of villages and indulged in wanton killing.

HISTORY FROM 1858 TO 1885

After the 1857 revolt, the British in February 1858, removed Haryana from the North Western Province and merged it with Punjab. The region of Haryana was divided into two divisions that of Hissar and Delhi. Delhi division consisted of the districts of Delhi, Gurgaon and Panipat while the Hissar division consisted of the districts of Hissar, Sirsa and Rohtak. The districts were further divided into tehsils, tehsils into Zails and Zails into villages. The Panjab government in 1871 ordered setting up of district committees or 'Zila Samiti'. The 1883 Panjab District Board Act gave more power to these Zila Samitis.

The formation of Arya Samaj on 10 April, 1875 was to play a very important role in the history of Haryana region.

The founder of Aryan Samaj, Swami Dayanand (1824-1883) was a great Sanskrit and Vedic scholar. Swami Dayanand came to Haryana in 1880.

He stayed in Rewari for some time to preach against superstition and illiteracy. He also established a branch of Arya Samaj in Rewari. Later another branch was established in Rohtak.

Later still, Lala Lajpat Rai played an important part in popularizing Arya Samaj in Haryana villages. Arya Samaj played a great role in removing backwardness in the farming community of Haryana, especially the Jats.

The formation of Congress party in 1885 speeded up the political activities in the Haryana region.

HISTORY FROM 1885 TO 1947

After the formation of Congress in 1885, the political activities in Haryana accelerated. In 1905, the British partitioned Bengal and this directly challenged the Congress program, which responded by the 'Swadeshi Andolan'. Sh. Murlidhar from Ambala and Lala Lajpat Rai in Hissar actively participated in this agitation. In October, 1907 in Ambala, a state level conference was held by the Congress. A large number of people from every corner of Punjab and Haryana participated in this conference.

Under the leadership of Lala Lajpat Rai, the conference decided to form branches in every district. Till this time the Congress's Swadeshi Andolan did not have much effect outside the urban middle class of the region. As a result of the Ambala conference decision, district level branches were formed in all the districts of Haryana and Punjab.

On 9 May 1907, the British exiled Lala Lajpat Rai to Burma causing a major setback to the activities of the Congress party. Due to increasing criticism, the British were forced to bring Lalaji back on 14 November 1907.

But the bitter fight between the Garam Dal and Naram Dal factions of the Congress resulted in its activities coming to a standstill. Due to this and various other reasons the agitation for independence ran out of steam and it remained so till the end of the First World War.

After the start of the First World War, the congress held a conference in Madras where it passed a resolution to support the British in its war effort. Four annual conferences were held by the Congress during the period of the war, and in each of them, similar resolutions for helping the British were passed. As a result congress workers from Haryana also started helping the British in their war effort. The main reason was that the leadership was in the hands of middle class urban people and they thought that by doing this they would be able to get some personal benefit.

During the war a very large number of Haryanavi youth got themselves enlisted in the army. In Rohtak district alone more that 20, 000 young men were recruited in the army by the British. Businessmen and other rich people donated large amounts of money to help the government. While the 'naram dal' faction of the congress was helping the British during the war, the 'garam dal' faction led by Bal Gangadhar Tilak and Ms. Annie Besant started the 'Home Rule League' agitation. In Haryana, Pt. Neki Ram Sharma was at the forefront of this agitation. After the Calcutta Adhiveshan in 1917, Tilakji asked Pt. Neki Ram Sharma to lead the Home Rule agitation in the Haryana region.

Pt. Neki Ram Sharma concentrated his activities particularly in the Rohtak region. Perturbed by this the Government threatened him with imprisonment and also tried to buy him out with offers of land and money, but to no avail. Disturbed by the failure of the Home Rule agitation he decided to invite Tilakji to Haryana but the Government reacted by banning Tilakji from coming to Punjab and arrested Pt. Neki Ram Sharma.

INDEPENDENT INDIA

On 1 November, 1966, Haryana was carved out of the mostly Hindi-speaking eastern portion of Punjab, while the mostly Punjabi-speaking western portion remained as current day Punjab. The city of Chandigarh, on the linguistic and physical border, was made a union territory to serve as capital of both these states. Chandigarh was due to transfer to state of Punjab in 1986, according to the Rajiv-Longowal Accord, but the transfer has been delayed pending an agreement on which parts of the Hindi speaking areas of Abohar and Fazilka, currently part of Firozpur District of Punjab, that should be transferred to Haryana in exchange. In the 1970s, Haryana contributed significantly to the Green Revolution and White Revolution in India.

2

Culture and Society

CULTURE

Haryana has its own unique traditional folk music, folk dances, saang (folk theater), cinema, belief system such as Jathera (ancestral worship), and arts such as Phulkari and Shisha embroidery.

Haryana is proud of a rich cultural heritage that goes way back to the Vedic times. The state is rich in folklore. The people of Haryana have their own traditions. The age old customs of meditation, Yoga and chanting of Vedic Mantras, are still observed by the masses. The seasonal and religious festivals glorify the culture of this region. The dance is said to be the mother of all arts. Music and poetry exist in tune, painting and architecture in space. The dance is just not a form of recreation but something needed to release the physical and emotional energy. Folk dances, like other creative art, helps in sublimating the performer's worries and cares.

Haryana has always been a state of diverse races, cultures and faiths. It is on this soil that they met and fused into something truly India. The people of Haryana have preserved their old religious and social traditions. They celebrate festivals with great enthusiasm and traditional fervour. Their culture and popular art are Saangs, dramas, ballads and songs in which they take great delight.

With Hindi, Punjabi, Urdu and English forming the main languages, there are numerous dialects which are spoken in Haryana. However, almost all of them have their base in Hindi with a smattering of Urdu and Panjabi thrown in.

Sanskrit is also taught in most of the schools in Haryana. In towns and cities, English is still to be adopted as the household lingo, but is spoken in a hazy mixture of Hindi.

The most striking feature of Haryana is its language itself; or rather, the manner in which it is spoken. Popularly known as Haryanavi, Bangaru or Jatu (language of Jats), it is perhaps a bit crude, but full of earthy humour and straightforwardness. With rapid urbanization, and due to Haryana's close proximity to Delhi, the cultural aspects are now taking a more modern hue.

FOLK THEATER AND DANCES

Folk music and dances of Haryana are based on satisfying cultural needs of primarily agrarian and martial natures of Haryanavi tribes.

Haryanvi musical folk theater main types are Saang, Rasa lila and Ragini. The Saang and Ragini form of theater was popularised by Lakhmi Chand.

Haryanvi folk dances and music have fast energetic movements. Three popular categories of dance are: festive-seasonal, devotional, and ceremonial-recreational. The festive-seasonal dances and songs are Gogaji/Gugga, Holi, Phaag, Sawan, Teej. The devotional dances and songs are Chaupaiya, Holi, Manjira, Ras Leela, Raginis). The ceremonial-recreational dances and songs are of following types: legendary bravery (Kissa and Ragini of male warriors and female Satis), love and romance (Been and its variant Nâginî dance, and Ragini), ceremonial (Dhamal Dance, Ghoomar, Jhoomar (male), Khoria, Loor, and Ragini).

FOLK DANCES-DHAMAL, LOOR, KHORIA, SANG

Ras Leela: This dance is common among the people living in the Faridabad district. In this dance the Gopis form a circle around lord Krishna.

Phag Dance: This is a seasonal dance of the farmers usually performed in the month of 'Phalgun'. This is a mixed dance but sometimes performed by men only. Women wear colourful traditional clothes and men display gay colourful turbans. The dance is accompanied by the beats of 'Tasha', 'Nagada', and 'Dhol'.

Loor: A well known dance of Haryana. It is performed around the Holi festival and is very popular in the Bangar. Girls usually participate in this dance wearing their traditional dress of 'Ghagra', 'Kurti', 'Chundri' and 'Chunda'.

Dhamal Dance: This is an ancient dance popular among the Ahirs of Gurgaon and Mahendergarh. The dance is performed outdoors by men on moonlit nights of Phalgun. They sing and dance to the sound of the Dhamal beats. At the start of the dance a long tune of 'Been' is played. It is said that the people perform this dance whenever their crop is ready for harvesting.

Gugga Dance: Gugga is worshipped all over Haryana. Gugga Pir is worshipped by both Hindus and Muslims. The dance is done in a procession held about a week before the Gugga naumi. The devotees sing and dance in praise of Gugga. The dance is accompanied by musical instruments like 'Deru', 'Thali' and 'Chimta'.

Jhumar Dance: This dance is performed exclusively by women. It takes its name from Jhumar, an ornament commonly worn on the forehead by young married women. The dance is performed to the beats of dholak and thali.

Ghumar Dance: It is a Rajasthani dance also popular in the area of Loharu, Dadri, Sirsa and Hissar. This is a religious dance and is performed by women devotees on their way to the temple. Women start dancing in a circle, then move to dancing in two rows and end up dancing in twos in a circle.

Khoria: This dance is popular in the central areas of Haryana. This dance is performed by women at the house of the bridegroom in the night on which the marriage party has gone to the bride's house. By this dance the women ask for the safe and sound return of the marriage party along with the newly wed couple. By staying awake whole night for this dance, they also protect their house since the men folk are all away to the bride's house. Due to the bawdy nature of this dance children are generally kept away.

Gangore Puja: Brass plates in their hands, girls make a circle and sing and dance.

Holi Dance: This dance is connected with the Holi festival of spring. It is performed with the accompaniment of drums and pipes. Both men and women participate. This dance is popular in the area of Faridabad, Palwal and Ballabhgarh.

Chhathi Dance: On the birth of a male child, this dance is performed on the sixth day of the birth by women. It is a romantic dance and performed at night. At the end of the celebration boiled wheat and chana are distributed.

Teej Dance: This dance is performed by women on the Teej festival. Women and girls enjoy themselves on outdoor swings and sing.

Saang: This is performed by a group of ten or twelve persons. They sing religious stories and folk tales in open spaces. It can be called a 'open air theatre'. The performance can continue for 5 hours. Some of the men dress as women to act and dance. 'Sang' or 'Swang' means a disguise or 'to impersonate'. This form of dance or drama was first started in its present form in about 1750 AD by Kishan Lal Bhaat.

Chaupaiya: This dance is performed by men wearing 'Dhoti', 'Kurtas' and colourful turbans. They dance to the beats of 'Manjiras', 'Chimta' and 'Nagadas'. Mostly performed while harvesting crops, this dance is based on songs having four lines or tetrameter hence called 'Chaupaiya'.

Folk music and songs

Haryanvi folk music are based on day to day themes and injecting earthy humor enlivens the feel of the songs. Haryanvi music takes two main forms: "Classical folk music" and "Desi Folk music" (Country Music of Haryana), and sung in the form of ballads and love, valor and bravery, harvest, happiness and pangs of parting of lovers.

Classical Haryanvi folk music

Classical Haryanvi folk music is based on Indian classical music. Hindustani classical ragas, learnt in gharana parampara of guru–shishya tradition, are used to sing songs of heroic bravery (such as Alha-Khand (1663-1202 CE) about bravery of Alha and Udal, Jaimal Fatta of Maharana Udai Singh II), Brahmas worship and festive seasonal songs (such as Teej, Holi and Phaag songs of Phalgun month near Holi).Bravery songs are sung in high pitch.

Desi Haryanvi folk music

Desi Haryanvi folk music (Haryanvi country folk music) The country-side or desi (native) form of Haryanvi music is based on Raag Bhairvi, Raag Bhairav, Raag Kafi, Raag Jaijaivanti, Raag Jhinjhoti and Raag Pahadi and used for celebrating community bonhomie to sing seasonal songs, ballads, ceremonial songs(wedding, etc.) and related religious legendary tales such as Puran Bhagat.

Relationship and songs celebrating love and life are sung in medium pitch. Ceremonial and religious songs are sung in low pitch. Young girls and women usually sing entertaining and fast seasonal, love, relationship and friendship related songs such as Phagan (song for eponymous season/month), Katak (songs for the eponymous season/month), Samman (songs for the eponymous season/month), bande-bandi (male-female duet songs), sathne (songs of sharing heartfelt feelings among female friends). Older women usually sing devotional Mangal Geet (auspicious songs) and ceremonial songs such as Bhajan, Bhat (wedding gift to the mother of bride or groom by her brother), Sagai, Ban (Hindu wedding ritual where pre-wedding festivities starts), Kuan-Poojan (a custom that is performed to welcome the birth of male child by worshiping the well or source of drinking water), Sanjhi and Holi festival.

Socially normative-cohesive impact

Music and dance for Haryanvi people is a great way of demolishing societal differences as folk singers are highly esteemed and they are sought after and invited for the events, ceremonies and special occasions regardless of their caste or status. These inter-caste songs are fluid in nature, and never personalized for any specific caste, and they are sung collectively by women from different strata, castes, dialects. These songs do transform fluidly in dialect, style, words, etc. This adoptive style can be seen from the adoption of tunes of Bollywood movie songs into Haryanvi songs. Despite this continuous fluid transforming nature, Haryanvi songs have a distinct style of their own as explained above.

Cuisine

81% people of Haryana are vegetarian, and cuisine of Haryana is based on fresh, earthy and wholesome ethos of its agrarian culture, where staples are roti, saag, vegetarian sabzi and abundance of milk products such as homemade nooni or tindi ghee, ghee (clarified butter), milk, lassi, kheer.

COLOURFUL CULTURE OF HARYANA

Haryana's culture is reflective of this colourful state. Submerged in the rich cultural heritage of Vedic Period, the mystical state of Haryana stands out from the crowd. Characterised by the hookahs and the charpoys, the vivid fairs and the swaying paddy fields; Haryana is one of the wealthiest states in India and is one of the most economically developed regions in South Asia. Popularly known as 'The Home of Gods', Haryana shares its borders with Rajasthan, Uttar Pradesh, Punjab, Himachal Pradesh and Delhi. This vibrant state has a bountiful culture, heritage, festivals, folklores and a vibrant landscape.

Some indispensable components of Haryana culture are-

CUISINE

The authentic cuisine of Haryana offers finger licking delicacies namely- Kachri ki Sabji, Churma, Malpuas, Bathua Raita, Meethi Gajar, Singhri ki Sabji, Meethe Chawal, Rabri and much more.

It will surely woo your heart and leave you with a lingering aftertaste, asking for more. The people of Haryana give a lot of importance to milk products like curd and lassi, and hence incorporate them in all their meals.

From time immemorial, Haryana has a tradition of preparing and distributing 'goond ladoos', prepared in desi ghee, on the arrival of a new born. Likewise, there is a range of 'choormas' that are served on specific occasions.

Some other traditional delicacies include paranthas with bathua raita, steamed rice with kadhi, khichri, kadai hara cholia and some different varieties of rotis like besan masala roti and bajra aloo roti.

Art and craft

Arts and crafts of Haryana comprise of the various forms of dance, music, pottery, embroidery, painting, weaving, sculpting, etc. The speciality is the very popular village handicrafts. Apart from being the major source of income for the craftsmen, these art forms are a super hit among tourists. The hues of pottery, the moulds of clay, the shimmer of handicrafts, the beads of terracotta; all combine to display the creative imagination of thousands of artists.

Like any other region of India, Haryana also has its traditional form of dance and music which is quite popular among people from all over the globe. The famous traditional dance forms include- Ghoomar, Gangaur and Khoria dance. The ancient folk music of Haryana is mainly of two types- classical and countryside.

Classical form belongs to the great legends while countryside music includes songs with varied ragas, sung in Hindustani style. These ragas comprise of Pahari style, Kafi, Bhairavi and Malhar style of music. Also, different types of musical instruments like Dholak, Drum, Matka, Harmonium, Damru, Shehnai, Manjira and Nagara, along with the Khanjri, Sarangi,

Tasha and Ghunguru, etc. are played during the singing and dancing festivals.

The handicraft manufacturers in Haryana offer a variety of arts and crafts including pottery making, exquisite furniture and woodcarving, handlooms, etc. Most popularly weaved handlooms are the shawls and durries. Haryana Shawls are very well-known because of the Phulkari, which has a great demand for its rich embroidery all over the globe.

Traditions and customs

Haryana has been a witness to a lot of hoary traditions and customs. It has emerged through the ravages of times and has still managed to hold on to many of its traditions- some good and some not so good. The natives of Haryana have always cherished a basic lifestyle with very frugal needs. Hence, it is in a state of perpetual conflict between hoary traditions and modern evolution.

The people of Haryana strictly adhere to their customs and cultural traditions. One such tradition is of meditation. Yoga and chanting of Vedic mantras have become an innate part of their lifestyle.

The dialect of Haryana, popularly known as Haryanvi, Bangaru or Jatu; is known to be a bit crude but is full of earthy humour and straightforwardness.

Most of the people of Haryana have more or less equal social status. The factor of age is a really dominating trait in Haryana, as all elders, whether rich or poor are treated with utmost respect and honour. Thus, it displays a very socialistic nature. In some parts of the state, economic status of an individual is also determined by the number of cattle he owns!

People here tend to retain their racial purity by not allowing marriages in the same gotra. Widow Remarriages are also not encouraged and it is hence a very big obligation to the community.

Apart from all the vibrant and earthy customs of Haryana, there are a lot of practices here which needs amendment at the earliest. The major among them are the denial of education to the girl child, female infanticide and practice of the purdah.

Traditional Dress

The vibrancy of the people of Haryana is quite evident in their lifestyle too. Their simplicity and spirited enthusiasm find expression in their way of dressing up.

Women of Haryana show a special affinity towards colours. Their basic trousseau includes Daaman, Kurti & Chunder. 'Chunder' is the long, coloured piece of cloth, decorated with shiny laces and motifs, and is meant to cover the head. 'Kurti' is a shirt like a blouse. The 'Daaman' is the flairy ankle-long skirt, in striking vibrant colours.

The men generally wear 'Dhoti', the wraparound cloth, tucked in between the legs with a white-coloured kurta worn on top of it. 'Pagri' is the traditional headgear for men, which is now worn mainly by the old villagers. All-white attire is a status symbol for men.

The culture of Haryana dates back to the Vedic times and the natives are known for their rich cultural heritage. Being a traditional society, the state has its own social beliefs and practices. Despite the influences from the Mughals and then the British, Haryana has retained its ancient heritage and continues to be the flag bearer of its traditions. From its ancient art forms to their traditional clothing and earthy lifestyle, we have a lot to gain from this enriching society.

LAND AND THE PEOPLE

Haryana pronunciation is a state in north India. It was carved out of the state of Punjab in 1966. It is bordered by Punjab and Himachal Pradesh to the north, and Rajasthan to the west and south. Eastern border to Uttarakhand & Uttar Pradesh is defined by river Yamuna. Haryana also surrounds Delhi on three sides, forming the northern, western and southern borders of Delhi. Consequently, a large area of Haryana is included in the National Capital Region.

The capital of Haryana is Chandigarh which is administered as a union territory and is also the capital of Punjab. The city of Gurgaon is emerging as a major hub for the information technology industry, it is a leading manufacturing hub as it is also home to Maruti Udyog Limited, India's largest automobile manufacturer, and Hero Honda Limited, the world's largest manufacturer of two-wheelers. Panipat, Panchkula and Faridabad are also industrial hubs .There is also an established steel and textile industry in the state.

Details: Haryana is primarily an agrarian state. The name itself means 'land covered with greenery' (The other meaning is where God comes, Hari-Aana). It is known for its wheat and milk production. In addition to the river Yamuna and Ghaggar, seasonal rivers such as the Markanda and Tangri pass through the state. Numerous irrigation canals that cross the state, bringing water for irrigation from the perennial rivers of the Himalayas.

The land is generally flat, covered with loamy soil and very suitable for agriculture. The southwestern area of the state is drier and sandier. There are some hilly areas, which form part of Siwalik Hills in the northeast and Aravalli Range in the south. The climate is continental, with extremes of heat in summer. Monsoon winds bring adequate rainfall between July and September.

Haryana has four universities and two medical colleges. The official language is Hindi and Punjabi is the second official language. A number of residents, especially rural, speak Haryanvi, a dialect of Hindi that is famous for its coarseness. Hinduism is followed by a majority of people, followed by Sikhism, Islam, Jainism and Christianity. Haryana was a part of both the Indus Valley Civilization and the early Vedic civilization. The Mahabharata referes to many locations which are now in Haryana such as Kurukshetra and Gurgaon.

The Ghagghar is now thought to be the original Saraswati River of Vedic times.

Divisions: The state is divided into four divisions for administrative purpose - Ambala, Rohtak, Gurgaon and Hisar. There are 20 districts, 47 subdivisions, 67 tehsils, 45 sub-tehsils and 116 blocks. Haryana has a total of 81 cities and towns. It has 6, 759 villages.

THE PEOPLE AGITATE FOR A SEPARATE STATE

The region of present day Haryana was made a part of Punjab in 1858 by the British. Due to the active role of people of Haryana in the revolt of 1857, this region was punished and no significant development work took place. The people of Haryana region were treated as second-class citizens. Moreover there were many differences between the people of these two regions like language, clothing and other habits. The demand for a separate state got a boost with the demand of Master Tara Singh for a 'Punjabi Suba' in 1948. Moreover there were problems between the Hindi-speaking and the Punjabi-speaking population.

To solve this problem the then Panjab Chief Minister, Sh. Bhimsen Sacchar introduced the 'Sacchar Formula' on 1 October 1949. According to this formula, the state was sub-divided into two parts: 1. Panjabi Area 2. Hindi Area. The Hindi Area included the districts of Rohtak, Hissar, Gurgaon, Kangra, Karnal and the tehsils of Jagadhari and Naraingarh. It was decided that the official language of the Punjabi area would be 'Panjabi' (Gurumukhi script) and the official language of the Hindi area would be Hindi (Devnagri script). The then state of PEPSU also decided to follow the same formula. But the 'Sacchar Formula' could not succeed and it became especially unpopular in the Hindi area.

On 25 December 1953, the Indian government set up a commission under the chairmanship of Syed Fiazal Ali for suggesting the reorganization of states according to language and culture. The proponents of 'Panjabi Suba' and Haryana both appeared before the Commission to press their case. But the Commission in its wisdom did not approve of the division or reorganization of Panjab. This decision of the commission caused great despondency in the region.

Panjab government tried to find a solution to this increasingly difficult problem by suggesting the division of the state into Panjabi speaking and Hindi speaking areas.

Accordingly, in April, 1956 the Indian government declared Panjab to be a dual-language state and divided it into 'Panjabi Area' and 'Hindi Area'. Both Hindi and Panjabi were declared its official language. The Hindi Area this time included the districts of Hissar, Rohtak, Karnal, Gurgaon, Mahendergarh, Shimla, Kangra, Kohistan and the tehsils of Ambala, Jagadhari, Naraingarh, Jind and Narwana. But in 1957, due to certain actions of Pratap Singh Kairon, the then Chief Minister of Panjab, this solution too failed.

The failure of this solution accelerated the demand for separate states in both the regions. In 1960 Master Tara Singh launched a 'Morcha' to press for his demand of 'Panjabi Suba'. He was promptly arrested on the orders of Panjab CM, P. S. Kairon. On the arrest of Master Tara Singh, Sant Fateh Singh took over the leadership of the agitation. Because Sant Fateh Singh was a secular person and well connected with the masses, he became more popular. He went on a 'Fast unto death' to force the government to accept their demand for the 'Panjabi Suba'. More than 57, 000 people went to jail in this 'Satyagrah'. Both the Indian and Panjab government were shaken by this agitation. The wily Panjab Chief Minister Kairon then played his trump card and released Master Tara Singh from jail.

Master Tara Singh was greatly disturbed by the increasing popularity of Sant Fateh Singh. He took the leadership of the agitation back from Sant Fateh Singh and persuaded him to break his fast. The he himself decided to go on a 'fast unto death', but broke the fast after 48 days. This caused Master Tara Singh to loose his popularity and Sant Fateh Singh became the leader of the Panjab people especially the Sikhs. Meanwhile discontent keep on simmering in the people of Haryana region for a separate state. In 1965, Sant Fateh Singh again decided to go on a fast on 10 August 1965 to press for the demand of the 'Panjabi Suba'. He further threatened self-immolation if the demand was not accepted in 25 days. The Hindus of the Panjabi Area opposed the demand for the division of the state fearing that they would be in a minority in the new state. The local press, which was also controlled by the Hindus, too joined in and openly opposed the division. The people of Haryana region, except for RSS and Jan Sangh followers, supported the demand for the division of Panjab into Hindi speaking and Panjabi speaking states.

Finally bowing to the growing pressure from the people of both the regions, the Indian government announced the setting up of a parliamentary committee for reorganization of Panjab on 23 September 1965. This committee was headed by Sardar Hukam Singh. Meanwhile in October, all the legislatures belonging to the Haryana region got together and discussed the issue of the new state. On 17 October 1965, in a big meeting in Rohtak, three important resolutions were passed:

A new *Hindi* speaking state should be formed, which shall include in addition to the Hindi speaking areas of *Punjab*, some areas of *Delhi*, *Rajasthan* and *Uttar Pradesh*.

If the states of Rajasthan and Uttar Pradesh are not agreeable, then the new state should be formed consisting of Hindi speaking areas of Panjab. The people of Haryana region would not tolerate any division of the Hindi speaking area and whole of this area should constitute the state of Haryana. Hukam Singh committee agreed to the division and reorganization of Panjab and recommended that a 'Boundary Commission' may be set up to facilitate this division. On 23 April, 1966, acting on the recommendation of the Hukam Singh Committee, the Indian government set up the Shah Commission under the chairmanship of Justice J. C. Shah, to divide and set up the boundaries of Punjab and Haryana.

A NEW STATE IS BORN

Haryana was carved out of the Indian state of Punjab on 1st November 1966. This state was formed on the recommendation of the Sardar Hukam Singh Parliamentary Committee. The formation of this committee was announced in the Parliament on 23 September 1965. On 23 April, 1966, acting on the recommendation of the Hukam Singh Committee, the Indian government set up the Shah Commission under the chairmanship of Justice J. C. Shah, to divide and set up the boundaries of Panjab and Haryana.

The commission gave its report on 31 May, 1966. According to this report the districts of Hissar, Mahendergarh, Gurgaon, Rohtak, and Karnal were to be a part of the new state of Haryana. Further the Tehsils of Jind (district Sangrur), Narwana (district Sangrur) Naraingarh, Ambala and Jagadhari were also included.

The commission recommended that Tehsil Kharar (including Chandigarh) should also be a part of Haryana. After receiving the report of the Shah Commission, the Indian government passed Panjab reorganization bill, 1966 on 18 September, 1966. According to this bill, the boundary of the Haryana was to be as follows:

The districts of Hissar, Rohtak, Gurgaon, Karnal and Mahendergarh.

The Jind and Narwana tehsils of Sangrur district.

The Ambala, Jagadhari and Naraingarh tehsils of Ambala district.

The Pinjore circle of Kharar tehsil (district Ambala).

Part of the Mani Majra circle of Kharar tehsil.

It was also decided that the two states of Haryana and Punjab would have a common High Court called the 'Panjab & Haryana High Court'. The other parts of the bill dealt with issues like division of the Parliament seats in Lok Sabha and Rajya Sabha.

IMPORTANT PLACES

Jagadhri: Known for utensils industry. Yugandhra & Ganadhari had been demolished by Nadirshah in 1739. The credit of rebuilding this city goes to Sardar Roa Singh in 1783. Slowly it became a major centre of metals industry.

Bhudia: A famous town situated 3 km away from Jagadhri and 8 km from Yamunanagar railway station. It is said that Hamayun came here for hunting in Shivalik forests made up a 'Rang-Mahal'. Many people guess the relation of 'Rang-Mahal' of Bhudia to Birbal, one of the Navrattana of Akbar. In nearby Dayalgarh, there is a very beautiful place of worship - the renovated old temple of Shree Pataleshvar Mahadev with a beautiful garden and some ashrams of saints made during mediaeval times.

Bilaspur and Kapalmochan: Bilaspur town, named after the writer of the Mahabharata - Maharishi 'Ved Vyas', is a historical place. It is supposed that there was an Ashram of Ved Vyas on the bank of a pond situated here. The statue of Uma Mahadev made in 9th-10th century, and statue of Ganesha made in 11th-12th century and remains of Gupta period prove the antecedence of Kapalmochan. People came from all parts of the country feel spiritual elevated by taking bath here in ponds (kunds) known as Rinmochan, Kapalmochan and Surya kund. There is also a Hindu temple and Gurudawara of Dasham Padhashahi.

Panchmukhi Hanuman Mandir: The temple is situated on the road coming from Bilaspur to Chhachhrauli, 4 km away from Bilaspur and it attracts large numbers of people.

Chhachrauli: The main tehsil situated in north east and 11 km from Jagadhri. In the past it was the capital of Kalsia state. Created by Raja Gurbaksh Singh in 1763. Today 'Ravi Mahal', Ghantaghar, Janak Niwas and the fort have their own dignity. There is also a Sainik Parivar Bhawan & Bal-kunj social welfare institution at Chhachrauli.

Ban Santur: This village is situated north east from Chhachhrauli near Kalesar - it is supposed to be connected with King 'Shantanu' of Mahabharata.

Adibadri: It lies 40 km north of Yamunanagar town. It is approached by road via Bilaspur and is about 2 kms. from the nearest village Kathgarh. Located in the foothills of the

Shivaliks, it is a picturesque location, abundant with natural beauty and tranquillity, with the Adi-Badri Narayana, Shri Kedar Nath and Mantra Devi Temples in the background. Three mounds of antiquities have recently been excavated by the Archaeological Survey of India.

Chaneti: It is situated 3 km away from Jagadhri. There is a grand Tomb of 8 meters in height made of bricks, in the area of about 100 sq. meters near the village. Made in round shape this is an old Buddhist Stupa. According to Hieun Tsang, this was built by the great King Ashoka.

Harnol and Topra: A religious place named 'Panjtirthi' is situated 15 km away from Yamunanagar on the road coming from Topra Kalan to Harnol. There are Shiv Temples and a Gurudwara which indicate the cordial relations of Sikhs and Hindus. People come here for sacred bath. There are statues of Lord Ram, Sita and five Pandavas.

Sadhaura: An old historical place. It was said that people coming from Haridwar and all the religious places of Himachal Pradesh used to take rest here. It was known as the 'Sadhu-raha' in the past. Later it became Sadhaura.

3

Government and Politics

GOVERNMENT OF HARYANA

The Government of Haryana, also known as the State Government of Haryana, or locally as the State Government, is the supreme governing authority of the Indian state of Haryana and its 22 districts. It consists of an executive, ceremonially led by the Governor of Haryana and otherwise by the Chief Minister, a judiciary, and a legislative branch.

Branches of government

Executive

As with other Indian states, the head of state of Haryana is the Governor, appointed by the President of India on the advice of the central government. His or her post is largely ceremonial. The Chief Minister is the head of government and is vested with most of the executive powers to run the 22 districts of Haryana across its six divisions.

Legislative

Chandigarh is the capital of Haryana and houses the Haryana Vidhan Sabha (Legislative Assembly) and the secretariat. The city also serves as the capital of Punjab, and is a union territory of India.

The present Legislative Assembly of Haryana is unicameral, consisting of 90 members of the legislative assembly (MLAs). Its term is five years, unless dissolved earlier.

Judicial

The Punjab and Haryana High Court, located in Chandigarh, has jurisdiction over the whole state.

HARYANA LEGISLATIVE ASSEMBLY

The Haryana Legislative Assembly or the Haryana Vidhan Sabha is the unicameral state legislature of Haryana state in northern India. The seat of the Vidhan Sabha is at Chandigarh, the capital of the state. The Vidhan Sabha comprises 90 Members of Legislative Assembly, directly elected from single-seat constituencies. The term of office is five years.

History

The body was founded in 1966, when the state was created from part of the state of Punjab, by the Punjab Reorganisation Act, 1966. The house initially had 54 seats, ten reserved for scheduled castes, this was increased to 81 seats in March 1967, and to 90 seats (including 17 reserved seats) in 1977.

POLITICS OF HARYANA

The key political players in Haryana state in northern India are the ruling Bharatiya Janata Party, the Indian National Congress, the Indian National Lok Dal, the Haryana Janhit Congress (BL) now is Haryana Janhit Congress Led by Pawan Pandit and his supporters after announcement of merger in Indian National Congress and the Bahujan Samaj Party.

National politics

There are 10 constituencies of the Lok Sabha (lower house in the Parliament of India). The Bhiwani-Mahendragarh constituency was announced to be formed in 2007 as result of the report by Delimitation Commission of India. The previous Bhiwani and Mahendragarh were merged to form this one.

State politics

The Haryana Legislative Assembly has 90 seats.

POLITICAL PARTIES

Ekta Shakti

Ekta Shakti (United Force), political party in Haryana, India, founded in 2004. The party president is Maratha Virender Verma, a former government employee. Verma is the son of Shiva Ram Verma, who was a minister of the erstwhile Bharatiya Jana Sangh.

Verma bases his political movement amongst a peasants caste called Rode.

Verma claims that the Rode caste descends from the Marathas, and through using the Maratha identity he was initially able to win some support from the community. Verma builds his political discourse on the accusation that northern Haryana would be discriminated against by politicians from western Haryana.

Verma was accused of having organized party activities whilst still in government service (which is illegal).

In the 2004 Lok Sabha elections the party launched three candidates from northern Haryana. They got 13 022, 82 430 and 31 202 votes.

Haryana Gana Parishad

Haryana Gana Parishad (Haryana Popular Association), a political party in Haryana, India. HGP was formed when Hissar Lok Sabha MP Jai Prakash was expelled from Haryana Vikas Party. HGP merged with Indian National Congress on April 8, 1999.

Haryana Nayay Party

Haryana Nayay Party is a political party in the Indian state of Haryana. It was formed on July 14, 2002 under the presidency of Ramanand Yadav, formerly the state general secretary of the Samajwadi Party in Haryana.

Haryana Republican Party

Haryana Republican Party, political party in the Indian state of Haryana. The party was founded on December 30, 2003 when the sole Republican Party of India member of the Haryana assembly, Karan Singh Dalal, broke away. On the same day Democratic Congress Party was founded as well.

Many saw HRP as a quasiparty, whose raison d'etre was to provide a loop-hole for the Anti-Defection Law as Dalal wanted to join Indian National Congress. After the Lok Sabha elections 2004 Dalal merged his HRP with Congress. But the speaker of the Haryana assembly reacted and suspended Dalal (and five other assembly members who had joined Congress) under the Anti-Defection Law. Thus the attempt on behalf of Congress to gain majority in the assembly failed.

Haryana State Akali Dal

Haryana State Akali Dal (or HSAD) is a Sikh political party in India, a splinter group of the Badal-led Shiromani Akali Dal that sided with Gurcharan Singh Tohra on the Ranjit Singh issue. HSAD was formed on May 23, 1999 on similar lines as Shiromani Akali Dal Delhi. Five out of eleven Shiromani Gurdwara Prabhandak Committee members from Haryana state joined HSAD. The HSAD general secretary is Kartar Singh Takkar.

Haryana Vikas Party

Haryana Vikas Party (Haryana Development Party) was a political party in the Indian state of Haryana. Its president was Bansi Lal and general secretary Surender Singh. On October

14, 2004 HVP merged with the Indian National Congress.

Manav Samaj Seva Party

Manav Samaj Seva Party (Human Society Service Party), is a political party in Haryana, India. MSSP was formed by the ex-president of the Bahujan Samaj Party Haryana state committee and MP, Aman Kumar Nagra, on May 12, 2002.

Samajik Ekta Party

Samajik Ekta Party (Social United Party), a political party in Haryana, India.

SEP president is Nafe Singh Dahiya. Ahead of the 1999 state assembly elections, SEP had joined the Haryana Sarvjatiya Morcha (Haryana All Caste Front).

Vishal Haryana Party

Vishal Haryana Party was a political party in the Indian state of Haryana, led by Rao Birender Singh. It merged with Congress (I) on September 23, 1978.

ADMINISTRATION

Divisions

The state is divided into 6 revenue divisions, 5 Police Ranges and 3 Police Commissionerates (c. January 2017). Six revenue divisions are: Ambala, Rohtak, Gurgaon, Hisar, Karnal and Faridabad.

Haryana has 10 municipal corporations (Gurigram, Faridabad, Ambala, Panchkula, Yamunanagar, Rohtak, Hisar, Panipat, Karnal and Sonepat), 18 municipal councils and 52 municipalities (c. Jan 2018).

Within these there are 22 districts, 72 sub-divisions, 93 tehsils, 50 sub-tehsils, 140 blocks, 154 cities and towns, 6,841 villages, 6212 villages panchayats and numerous smaller dhanis.

Districts

Divisions	Districts
Ambala	Ambala, Kurukshetra, Panchkula, Yamuna Nagar
Faridabad	Faridabad, Palwal, Nuh
Gurgaon	Gurgaon, Mahendragarh, Rewari,
Hisar	Fatehabad, Jind, Hisar, Sirsa,
Rohtak	Jhajjar, Charkhi Dadri, Rohtak, Sonipat, Bhiwani
Karnal	Karnal, Panipat, Kaithal

Law and order

Haryana Police force is the law enforcement agency of Haryana. Five Police Ranges are Ambala, Hissar, Karnal, Rewari and Rohtak. Three Police Commissionerates are Faridabad, Gurgaon and Panchkula. Cybercrime investigation cell is based in Gurgaon's Sector 51.

The highest judicial authority in the state is the Punjab and Haryana High Court, with next higher right of appeal to Supreme Court of India. Haryana uses e-filing facility.

Governance and e-governance

The Common Service Centres (CSCs) have been upgraded in all districts to offer hundreds of e-services to citizens, including application of new water connection, sewer connection, electricity bill collection, ration card member registration, result of HBSE, admit cards for board examinations, online admission form for government colleges, long route booking of buses, admission forms for Kurukshetra University and HUDA plots status inquiry. Haryana has become the first state to implement Aadhaar-enabled birth registration in all the districts. Thousands of all traditional offline state and central government services are also available 24/7 online through single unified UMANG app and portal as part of Digital India initiative.

4

Language and Literature

LANGUAGES

Languages of Haryana (2001)

Hindi (87.31%)

Punjabi (10.57%)

Urdu (1.23%)

Bengali (0.19%)

Nepali (0.10%)

Others (0.60%)

Hindi was the sole official language of Haryana till 2010 and it is spoken by the majority of the population (87.31%). Haryana has 70% rural population who primarily speak Haryanvi dialect of Hindi, as well as other related dialects, such as Bagri and Mewati.

LANGUAGES OF HARYANA

The main languages spoken by the people of Haryana are Haryanvi, Hindi, Punjabi, Urdu and English. Many dialects have originated, which are spoken throughout the length and breadth of Haryana. However, almost all of them have their base in Hindi with a smattering of Urdu and Panjabi thrown in for good measure.

In towns and cities, English is still to be adopted as the household language. It is spoken in a hazy mixture of Hindi. The most striking feature of Haryana is its language itself; or rather, the manner in which it is spoken. Popularly known as 'Haryanvi' (or as Bangaru or Jatu), it is actually a bit crude.

LANGUAGE AND LITERATURE

Urdu: Urdu is an Indo-European language which originated in India, most likely in the vicinity of Delhi from where it spread to the rest of the subcontinent. Urdu along with Hindi forming the Hindustani language is the second most popular 'first' language and second most popular 'first or second' language in the world. Urdu by itself is the twentieth most popular 'first' language in the world. It developed from the interaction between local Indian Sanskrit-derived Prakrits and the Persian languages. This process took place mostly in military camps, and word Urdu means "army" or "horde" in Turkish.

It soon became the language of the Mughals, distinguished linguistically from local languages by its large and extensive Persian-Arabic vocabulary superimposed on a native Hindi base of grammar, usages and vocabulary. The result was what has been considered by some to be one of the world's most beautiful languages, the "Kohinoor" ("Mountain of Light," a famed native, large and brilliant diamond) of India. It is widely spoken today in both India and Pakistan and all countries having a sizeable South Asian Diaspora.

History: There are different views on the origins of Urdu, differing in both time and geographic location. Urdu may have originated anywhere in India: the Deccan, in Punjab, in Sindh or in the neighborhood of Delhi. These hypothesis are backed by Urdu literature having been found in these areas as far back as the period of the Delhi Sultanate. Keeping in mind the linguistic character of the areas around Delhi, it is said that Urdu originated in or around Delhi over a period of a few centuries.

A continuous progression is seen in linguistic development from Sanskrit to the modern languages of Northern India, though there is a strong link between the Prakritic language 'Hindvi' of the middle ages and Urdu of today. The works of Amir Khusrau are intelligible to the speakers of Urdu and Hindi, even though they were written in the 14th century. It is hypothesized that Urdu developed when a regular and slow stream of Persian and Arabic words were infused into the language Hindvi.

Urdu has been known by a host of names during this seven century long interval: Hindvi, Hindi (not to be confused with modern Hindi), Rekhta, Shahjahani, Deccani and Urdu-e-Mualla. There is some debate as to whether all of them represent the same language, but the majority of experts agree that these are names of the language known today as Urdu.

Although the language originated near Delhi, it was in the Deccan that it first gained acceptance. The rulers of the Deccan were supportive of local languages, opposing the Persian influence in northern India. In the Deccan, the court became the centre for the development of Urdu, and the initial poetry and literature in Urdu comes from there. The idea of using Urdu rather than Persian as the media of poetry and literature eventually spread to the northern parts of the Indian subcontinent.

After the mainstream acceptance of Urdu as a poetic language in North India, a large number of poets began writing in it. Great poets such as Mir, Sauda, Ghalib, Zauq and Haali made the language acceptable as a literary medium. The increasing quantity of poetry and literature caused the language to become more uniform and less volatile than it had been in the past.

Classification and Related Languages: Urdu is a member of the Hindustani group of languages, which is a subgroup of the Indo Aryan group, which is in turn part of the Indo European family of languages. Urdu is related to most of the languages of India and northern South Asia, all of them having similar grammatical structures and a certain common vocabulary. The Punjabi language is very similar to Urdu. Written Punjabi (in Shahmukhi script) can be understood by speakers of Urdu, with a little difficulty, but spoken Punjabi has a different phonology and cannot be easily understood by Urdu speakers. The closest linked language to Urdu is Hindi.

GEOGRAPHIC DISTRIBUTION OF URDU SPEAKERS

In India, Urdu is spoken as a mother tongue by many in the central and northern states like Uttar Pradesh and Delhi. In Haryana it is spoken in the Mewat area as well as many of the urban areas. While in India, Muslims might be seen as tending to identify with Urdu; Hindus and Sikhs naturally speak Urdu regardless of religion, especially when they have grown up in such traditional Urdu-strongholds such as Lucknow and Hyderabad. Some would contend that the brand of Hindi spoken in Bollywood film is in fact closer to Urdu than Hindi, especially in filmi songs.

In Pakistan, Urdu is spoken as a mother tongue by a majority of people such cities as Karachi and Hyderabad in the southern province of Sindh. In spite of its status as the national language, only 8% of Pakistanis speak Urdu as their first language, with about 48% speaking Punjabi. As time goes by, more and more Pakistanis of Punjabi or other background are speaking Urdu as a first language. It is evident that the number of native Urdu speakers is increasing quickly in urban centres. Apart from the Indian subcontinent, Urdu is also spoken in urban Afghanistan. It is also spoken to some extent in the major urban centres in the Persian Gulf countries. Urdu is also spoken by a large number of people in the major urban centres of the UK, the USA, Canada and Australia. Urdu is the sole official language of Pakistan, although English is used in most elite circles and Punjabi has plurality of native speakers.

Urdu is one of the official languages of India, and while the government school system emphasizes Hindi, many universities, especially in Lucknow, Uttar Pradesh, continue to foster Urdu as a language of prestige and learning. In the Indian state of Jammu & Kashmir, Urdu is the official language.

Grammar: Urdu nouns fall into two grammatical genders : masculine and feminine. Although there is disagreement over the gender of some words, particularly words newly introduced from English which do not have genders. In Urdu there is also the presence of either a singular or a plural state.

Politeness: A host of words are used to show respect and politeness. These words are generally used with people who are older in age or with whom you are not acquainted. For example the English word 'you' can be translated into three words in Urdu 'tu' (informal, extremely intimate, or derogatory) 'tum' (informal) and 'aap' (formal and respectful).

Vocabulary: Urdu has a very rich vocabulary with words from Indian languages and Persian. Urdu language is dominated by words from Hindi, Sanskrit, Persian and Arabic. One count placed the number of Hindi-Prakrit words in the vocabulary at about 60% with the remaining 40% comprising Arabic-Persian words. There are also a number of borrowings from Turkish, Portuguese and English. Many of the Arabic words that have found a place in the Urdu Language, often through the conduit of Persian, have differently nuanced meanings and usages.

Writing System: Urdu is written in a derivative of the Persian alphabet which is itself derivative of the Arabic alphabet. It is read from right to left. Urdu is similar in appearance and letters to Persian and Pashto. Urdu differs in appearance from Arabic in that it uses the more complex and sinuous nastaliq script whereas Arabic tends to the more modern naskh. Nastaliq is notoriously difficult to typeset, so Urdu newspapers are made from hand-written masters. Although the styles are different, people who can read Urdu can read Arabic, as Arabic uses the same alphabet but with fewer letters.

URDU-HINDI-HINDUSTANI

Urdu, Hindi and the consequent Hindustani language have a complex relationship with each other. Urdu and Hindi have been called different languages on the one hand and dialects of the same language on the other. Hindustani is generally thought of as the language that encompasses both Urdu and Hindi and forms the mother language of these two languages. The most major difference between Urdu and Hindi is that Urdu is written in the Nasta'liq font of the modified Arabic script while Hindi is written in the Devanagari script.

Urdu, Hindi and Hindustani are all segments on a long linguistic chain. At one end is a heavily Persianized language which is written in the Nasta'liq font and in a modified Arabic script. At the other end is a heavily Sanskritized language which is written in the Devanagari form. The progression from one to the other is continuous and slow.

The basic grammars are the same. The words are replaced either by more Sanskritized or more Persianized forms. Urdu forms the segment of the chain more towards the Persian side and Hindi forms the segment of the chain more towards the Sanskrit side. The language spoken in the north of the Indian subcontinent is basically halfway between the two extremes and represents Hindustani.

Despite this, the casual spoken languages are similar and in some cases not even distinguishable. For example, it is said that Indian movies (primarily of Bollywood) are made in Hindi, but the language used in many of these movies is similar to Urdu spoken in Pakistan. On the other hand, Pakistani TV dramas are made in Urdu, and yet the language used in these dramas is similar to the language used by Hindi speakers in India.

LITERATURE

Urdu has been used as a language for literature for a short period of time. Persian being the language of choice until recently.

But even so a varied and extensive literature of the language has come up. A large number of volumes of Islamic works are present in Urdu. Two genres have seen a lot of development in Urdu. The Daastaan is a long long story which might include multiple story lines, plots and may not have any particular focus but it had the usage of beautiful linguistic structures, it is not used any more.

The Afsaana is a short story. It has come to become the primary genre of Urdu literature. The most well known Afsana writers or Afsana Nigaar in Urdu are Saadat Hasan Manto, Ahmed Nadeem Qasmi, Munshi Premchand and Krishan Chander. Munshi Premchand, a Hindu writer, became known as a pioneer in the Afsana, though some contend his were not technically the first, and showed that religion was not a bar to Urdu's grand capacity to express.

Poetry: Urdu is very well known for its beautiful Urdu poetry. Urdu was the premiere language of poetry in India for two centuries and has a large and rich collection of poetry in a host of different poetic forms. The Ghazal is a form of poetry that was used extensively by poets all over South Asia.

But its beauty and grace has made it well liked by people from all faiths all over the region. Mir, Ghalib, Faiz and Haali are some of the premiere poets in the genre of Ghazal. In addition to Ghazal, the poetic forms of Rubai, Masnavi, Qaseeda, Geet, Marsia, Shehr aashob, Doha and Nauha are very well developed in Urdu. Foreign forms such as Sonnet and Haiku have also been used by Urdu poets, mainly in the modern era.

Sanskrit is the earliest attested members of the Indo-European language family, and an official language of India. Hindi, the main official language of India, has descended from Sanskrit. Seen by many as the Asian equivalent of Latin, its vast religious and literary tradition is most famously seen in its Hindu or Vedic traditions. The first Sanskrit text available is the Rig Veda, from the early canon of Vedic culture Hinduism. Far more Sanskrit texts are preserved than those in Latin and Greek combined. All well known ancient Hindu texts like, Vedas, Bhagvad-Gita, Mahabharata, Upanishads, Vedanta and Ayurveda, were written in some form of Sanskrit.

History: The word Sanskrit means completed, refined, perfected. Sam (together) + krtam (created). Virtually every Sanskrit student in India learns the story that Sanskrit was created and then refined over many generations (traditionally more than a thousand years) until it was considered complete and perfect. When the term arose in India, 'Sanskrit' was not conceived of as referring to a specific language set apart from other languages (the people of the time regarded languages more as dialects), but rather referred to a particularly refined manner of speaking.

The knowledge of Sanskrit was a marker of social class and educational attainment, and was closely governed by the analyses of grammarians. This form of the language evolved out of the earlier "Vedic" form, and scholars often distinguish Vedic from Classical as separate languages. However, they are extremely similar in most regards, differing only in a few points of phonology, vocabulary, and grammar.

Vedic is the language of the Vedas, the earliest sacred texts of India and the base of the Hindu religion. The earliest of the Vedas, the Rig Veda, was composed in 2nd millennium BC. The Vedic form survived until the middle of the first millennium BC. It is around this time that Sanskrit made the transition from a first language to a second language of religion and learning, marking the beginning of the Classical period. A form of Sanskrit called Epic Sanskrit is seen in the Mahabharata and other Hindu epics. This includes more *prakritisms* (borrowings from common speech) than Classical Sanskrit proper. There is also a language dubbed *Buddhist Hybrid Sanskrit* by scholars, which is actually a prakrit ornamented with Sanskritized elements, perhaps for purposes of ostentation.

There is a strong genetic relationship between the various forms of Sanskrit and the Middle Indo-Aryan "Prakrits", or vernacular languages, (in which, among other things, most early Buddhist texts are written) and the modern Indo-Aryan languages. The Prakrits are probably descended from Vedic, and there is mutual interchange between later forms of Sanskrit and various Prakrits. There has also been reciprocal influence between Sanskrit and the Dravidian languages.

The Vedic form of Sanskrit is a close descendant of Proto-Indo-European, the reconstructed root of all later Indo-European languages. Vedic Sanskrit is the oldest attested language of the Indo-Iranian branch of the Indo-European family. It is very closely related to *Avestan*, the language of Zoroastrianism. The genetic relationship of Sanskrit to modern European languages and classical Greek and Latin can be seen in cognates like mother and matr or father and pitr. Other interesting links are to be found between Sanskritic roots and Persian, present in such a striking example as the generic term for 'land' which in Sanskrit is sthaan and in Persian staan.

European scholarship in Sanskrit, initiated by Heinrich Roth and Johann Ernest Hanxleden, led to the proposal of the Indo-European language family by Sir William Jones, and thus played an important role in the development of Western linguistics. Indeed, linguistics (along with phonology, etc.) first arose among Indian grammarians who were attempting to catalog and codify Sanskrit's rules. Modern linguistics owes a great deal to these grammarians, and to this day, key terms for compound analysis are taken from Sanskrit. The oldest surviving Sanskrit grammar is Pânini's c. 500 BC.

PANINI AND ASHTADHYAYI

Arguably, no grammarian has had as much influence over the grammar of any language as much as Panini has had over Sanskrit grammar and phonetics. Panini was a Vaishnav grammarian from approximately the 5th cent BC. The Ashtadhyayi was his magnum-opus. The book completely standardized Sanskrit grammar and phonetics. Panini's grammar became widely accepted and is still the standard (a common way to classify ancient Sanskrit books is to classify them as Pre-Panini or Post-Panini).

However, Panini's stroke of brilliance lies in the fact that the grammar he wrote, in addition to being a descriptive grammar, is also a generative grammar. Panini used metarules, transformations, and recursion in such sophistication that his grammar has the computing power equivalent to a Turing machine.

The Backus-Naur Form or BNF grammars used to describe modern programming languages have significant similarities with Panini's grammar rules. In applying his rules to Sanskrit verse he used such texts as the Hindu Shiva Sutras, thereby establishing principles of harmony and linguistic wholeness.

SANSKRIT PLAYS

Theatre, as an art was introduced by the Greeks after the attempted invasion of India in 326 BC by Alexander the Great. This is reflected in the fact that the Sanskrit word for Curtain is Yavanika, which is derived from the word Yavana, Sanskrit for Greek (the word Yavana is a distortion of Ionia. Most of the soldiers in Alexander's army were from Ionia, a province in Ancient Greece).

Most of the Sanskrit plays were written between the 2nd cent BC and the 7th cent AD. Though originally inspired by Greek theatre, Sanskrit plays are completely different from their Greek counterparts; the most famous Greek plays are tragedies, while almost all Sanskrit plays are romantic, funny or both. Reflective, possibly, of the opulent and carefree lifestyle of India's classical or Golden age (3rd-7th cents AD). Though numerous plays written in this period are still available, precious little is known about the authors themselves. This is mainly because of the reticence that Sanskrit writers displayed about writing about themselves in their forewords. Most of the information about these playwrights has been available by the references made to the writers by other writers of the same or later periods.

Mriccha Katika (The clay cart): One of the earliest Sanskrit plays, this is thought to have been composed by Shudraka in the 2nd cent BC. Rife with romance, sex, royal intrigue and comedy, the juicy plot of the play has numerous twists and turns. The main story is about a middle-class person, Charudatta, and his love for a rich courtesan, Vasantasena. The love affair is complicated by a royal courtier, who is also attracted to Vasantasena. The plot is further complicated by thieves and mistaken identities, and is hilarious and entertaining (a particularly hilarious scene has a thief, who is trying to dig a hole in the wall of a house to break in, wondering about whether the hole should be circular or triangular). The play was made into a 1984 Bollywood movie Utsav, directed by Girish Karnad.

Bhasa's Plays: The plays written by Bhasa were only known to historians through the references of later writers, the manuscripts themselves being lost. Manuscripts of 13 plays written by him were discovered in an old library in 1913 by the scholar Ganapati Shastry. A 14th play was later discovered and attributed to Bhasa, but its authorship is disputed.

Bhasa's most famous plays are Svapna Vasavadattam (Vasavadatta's dream) and Pratijna Yaugandharayaanam (The vows of Yaugandharayana). Bhasa is considered to be one of the best Sanskrit playwrights, next only to Kalidasa.

Kalidasa: Kalidasa (3rd-4th AD) is easily the greatest poet and playwright in Sanskrit, and occupies the same position in Sanskrit literature that Shakespeare occupies in English literature. He deals primarily with famous Hindu legends and themes; three famous plays by Kalidasa are Vikramorvashiyam (Vikrama and Urvashi), Malakavi-kagnimitram (Malavika and Agnimitra), and the play that he is most known for: Abhijnana Shakuntalam (The Recognition of Shakuntala). The last named play is considered to be a perfect play in Sanskrit. More than a millenium later, it would so powerfully impress the famous German writer Goethe that he would write:

"Wouldst thou the young year's blossoms and the fruits of its decline

And all by which the soul is charmed, enraptured, feasted, fed,

Wouldst thou the earth and heaven itself in one sole name combine?

I name thee, *O Sakuntala!* and all at once is said. "

Kalidasa also wrote two large epics, Raghuvamsham (The Genealogy of Raghu) and Kumarasambhavam (Birth of Kumara), and two smaller epics, Ritusamhaara (Medley of Seasons) and Meghadutam (The Cloud Messenger), another 'perfect' work. Kalidasa's writing is characterized by the usage of simple but beautiful Sanskrit, and by his extensive use of similes. His similes have earned him the saying, Upama Kalidasasya (Kalidasa owns simile).

Other important plays written in this period include Ratnavali and Nagananda, by Sri Harsha in the 7th century.

BHARATA'S NATYA SHASTRA

The NatyaShastra (Scripture of Dance) is a keystone work in Sanskrit literature. Again almost nothing is known about its author, Bharata. Bharata is also the name of a character in Hindu mythology; the author of the Natyashastra bears no relationship to the mythological character.

The Natya Shastra deals with the different arts used to express one's feelings: primarily music, dance, literature and theatre. Bharata laid down broad guidelines for the way these arts are and should be expressed.

The Natya Shastra came to be widely followed, and is thus the foundation of the fine arts in India. Among other things, the book gave a foundation to the concept of Rasa, or emotions that find artistic expression. Bharata identified nine Rasas: Adbhuta

(Wonder), Hasya (Laughter), Shringara (Love), Shaanta (Peace), Bibhatsa (Disgust), Vira (Valour), Karuna (Pathos), Bhaya (Fear) and Raudra (Anger).

Classical Poetry: This refers to the poetry produced from the 3rd to approximately the 7th centuries. Kalidasa is the foremost example of a classical poet. While Kalidasa's Sanskrit usage is simple but beautiful, later Sanskrit poetry shifted towards highly stylized literary accents: stanzas that read the same backwards and forwards, words that can be split in different ways to produce different meanings, sophisticated metaphors, and so on. A classic example is the poet Bharavi and his magnum opus, the Kiratarjuniya (6th-7th century).

The greatest works of poetry in this period are the five Mahakavyas, or great epics:

- Kumarasambhavam by Kalidasa
- Raghuvamsham by Kalidasa
- Kiratarjuniya by Bharavi
- Shishupala Vadha by Sri Maagha
- Naishadiya Charitam by Sri Harsha

Other major literary works from this period are Kadambari by Bana Bhatta, the first Sanskrit novelist (6th-7th centuries), and Kama Sutra by Vatsyayana.

LATER SANSKRIT LITERATURE

Some important works from the 11th century:

- Katha-Saritsagara (An Ocean of Stories) by Somadeva; this was a poetic adaptation in Sanskrit of Brihat-katha, written in the 5th cent BC in the Paishachi dialect. The Paishachi manuscript of the Brihat-katha has not been found. The thousands of short stories embedded in this book inspired numerous later stories, most notably several stories of the Arabian Nights (note that the Arabian Nights was first compiled in the 9th century and that this book was written only in the 11th cent. However, the stories in this book have existed since the 5th cent BC). One of the famous series of stories in this work is the Vikram and Betal series, known to every child in India.

- Geeta Govinda (The song of Govinda) by Jayadeva; this is the story of Lord Krishna's love for Radha, and is written in beautiful and musical Sanskrit. A central text for Hindu sects in the East, it is still recited regularly in the major Hindu pilgrimage Jagannath Mandir, located in Puri, Orissa.

Beyond the 11th century, the use of Sanskrit for general literature declined, importantly because of the emergence of literature in vernacular Indian languages (notably Hindi, Marathi, Tamil and Kannada). Sanskrit continued to be used for largely Hindu religious and philosophical literature. Sanskrit literature also fueled literature in vernacular languages, and the Sanskrit language itself continued to have a profound influence over the development of Indian literature in general.

HINDI

Hindi is a language spoken in most states in northern and central India. It is an Indo-European language, of the Indo-Iranian subfamily. It evolved from the Middle Indo-Aryan prakrit languages of the middle ages, and indirectly, from Sanskrit. Hindi derives a lot of its higher vocabulary from Sanskrit. Due to Muslim influence in northern India, there are also a number of Persian and Turkish loanwords.

Linguists think of Hindi and Urdu as the same language, the difference being that Hindi is written in Devanagari and draws vocabulary from Sanskrit, while Urdu is written in Arabic script and draws on Persian. The separation is largely a political one; before the partition of India into India and Pakistan, spoken Hindi and Urdu were considered the same language, Hindustani. Since partition, Standard Hindi has developed by replacing many words of Persian origin with Sanskrit words. Hindi and Urdu presently have four standard literary forms: Standard Hindi, Urdu, Dakkhini (Dakhini), and Rehkta. Dakhini is a dialect of Urdu from the Deccan region of south-central India, chiefly from Hyderabad, that uses fewer Persian words. Rehkta is a form of Urdu used chiefly for poetry.

After Chinese, Hindi is the second most spoken language in the world. About 500 million people speak Hindi, in India and abroad, and the total number of people who can understand the language may be 800 million. A 1997 survey found that 66% of all Indians can speak Hindi, and 77% of the Indians regard Hindi as '*one language across the nation*'. More than 180 million people in India regard Hindi as their mother tongue. Another 300 million use it as second language.

Outside of India, Hindi speakers are 100,000 in USA; 685,170 in Mauritius; 890,292 in South Africa; 232,760 in Yemen; 147,000 in Uganda; 5,000 in Singapore; 20,000 in New Zealand; 30,000 in Germany. Urdu, the official language of Pakistan, is spoken by about 41 million in Pakistan and other countries. Hindi became one of the official languages of India on January 26, 1965 and it is a minority language in a number of countries, including Fiji, Mauritius, Guyana, Suriname, Trinidad and Tobago, and United Arab Emirates.

Hindi is generally classified in the Central Zone of the Indo-Aryan languages. Khadiboli, the dialect spoken in Western Uttar Pradesh, east of Delhi is the basis for the language used by the government and taught in schools. Hindi is the predominant language in the states and territories of Himachal Pradesh, Delhi, Haryana, Chandigarh, Uttar Pradesh, Rajasthan, Madhya Pradesh, Bihar, as well as the cities of Mumbai and Hyderabad.

Is not easy to delimit the borders of the Hindi speaking region. A number of spoken languages are very closely related to Hindi, and may be considered dialects, including Bambaiya Hindi, Bhaya, Braj, Braj Bhasha, Bundeli, Chamari, Ghera, Gowli, Haryanvi, Kanauji, and others.

Some of the East-Central Zone languages, including Awadhi (Avadhi), Bagheli, Chhattisgarhi and Dhanwar, and Rajasthani languages, including Marwari, are also widely considered to be dialects of Hindi. There has been considerable controversy on the status of Punjabi and the Bihari languages, including Maithili, Bhojpuri, and Magadhi.

Hindi's popularity has been helped by *Bollywood*, the Hindi film industry. These movies have an international appeal and now they have broken into the Western markets as well. The beginnings of Hindi literature go back to the Prakrits that are a part of the classical Sanskrit plays. Tulasidas's Ramacharitamanas attained wide popularity. Modern masters include Sumitra Nandan Pant, Maithili Sharan Gupta, Mahadevi Varma, Ajneya.

Punjabi: Punjabi (also spelled Panjabi) is the language of the Punjab regions of India and Pakistan. It is an Indo-European language of the Indo-Iranian subfamily. Also, as an adjective, the word Punjabi qualifies anything or anyone that is related to either Punjab or the Punjabi language, such as the speakers of Punjabi, inhabitants of Punjab or the Punjabi cuisine of the region.

Punjabi is the official language of the Indian state of Punjab, and is also spoken in neighboring areas such as Haryana and Delhi. In Pakistan however, Urdu is the official language and Punjabi has no official status in education.

In formal contexts, such as government, newspapers, and education, as well as in most writing, Pakistani Punjabi speakers tend to use Urdu and English, which are the nation's official tongues. This has led to resentment from many Punjabi speakers, who form the largest single linguistic group in Pakistan.

Punjabi is also spoken as a minority language in several other countries, including Afghanistan, as well as many nations where Punjabis have emigrated in large numbers, such as Britain, Canada, and the United States.

Punjabi is the sacred language of the Sikhs, in which the religious literature is written. It is the usual language of Bhangra music, which has recently gained wide popularity both in South Asia and abroad.

Punjabi culture, much like its Bengali counterpart, suffered a split between India and Pakistan during the Partition of 1947. As such, Punjabi language and culture tend to be uniting factors in spite of national and religious affiliations.

Modern Punjabi has borrowed extensively from other languages, including Hindi, Urdu, Persian and English. Like other North Indian languages, is derived from Sanskrit and is therefore Indo-European.

In addition, like Hindi and Urdu, it has a substantial number of loanwords from Persian, and even a few from Turkish. Many sources subdivide the Punjabi language into Western Punjabi (Lahnda) and Eastern Punjabi.

There are several scripts used for writing the Punjabi language, depending on the region and the dialect spoken, as well as the religion of the speaker.

Sikhs and others in the Indian state of Punjab tend to use the Gurumukhi or Gurmukhi (from the mouth of the Gurus) script.

Hindus, and those living in neighboring states such as Haryana, Himachal Pradesh and Delhi sometimes use the Devanagari script. Muslims and Pakistani Punjabis, use a modified Arabic script called Shahmukhi.

Much like English, Punjabi has moved around the world and developed local forms by integrating local vocabulary. While most loanwords come from English, Hindi and Urdu (and indirectly, from Persian), Punjabis around the world have integrated terms from such languages as Spanish and Dutch. A distinctive "Diaspora Punjabi" is thus emerging.

PHONOLOGY AND WRITING SYSTEM

Sanskrit has 48 phonemes (Vedic Sanskrit has 49). The Sanskrit syllabary serves as a model for most Indian language writing systems, including Hindi, except Urdu and those of the southern base, like Tamil and Malayalam. The sounds are described here in their traditional order: vowels, stops and nasals (starting in the back of the mouth and moving forward), and finally the liquids and sibilants. (Note: The long vowels are held about twice as long as their short counterparts. Also, there exists a third, extra-long length for most vowels, which is used in various cases, but particularly when recording a shout, or a greeting.)

It also has four semivowels: y, r, l, v. All of these but r have nasalized forms. Sanskrit also has palatal, retroflex, and alveolar sibilants. Rounding out the consonants are the voiced and voiceless h (the voiceless h, called the *visarga*, tends to repeat the preceding vowel after itself) and the *anusvaara*, which often appears as nasalization of the preceding vowel or as a nasal homorganic to the following consonant. Vedic Sanskrit had a pitch or tonal accent, but it was lost by the Classical period. Vedic Sanskrit also had labial and velar fricatives and a retroflex L.

Sandhi: Sanskrit has an elaborate set of phonological rules called *Sandhi* and samaas which are expressed in its writing (except in so-called pada texts). Sandhi reflects the sort of blurring that occurs in combining sounds, particularly at word-boundaries; this occurs in spoken language generally, but is explicitly codified in Sanskrit. A simple example of English sandhi is "an apple" versus "a clock". Sandhi can make Sanskrit difficult for the inexperienced reader. It also creates ambiguities which clever writers have exploited to perform such feats as writing poems which can be interpreted in multiple, conflicting ways depending on how the reader chooses to break apart the sandhi.

Script: Sanskrit historically has had no single script associated with it. For instance, the ancient Brahmi characters were used by Ashoka for his pillar inscriptions. Later, *Grantha* was used, as were other scripts such as Kannada in the South, and Bengali and other north Indian scripts in other regions.

However, over many years, and especially recently, the syllabic Devanagari (meaning "as used in the city of the Gods") script has become the most widely used and associated with Sanskrit. Occasionally, in regions of India where Devnagri is not the script of the vernacular (as it is with Hindi or Marathi) one will find texts still written in the local script, such as Grantha in the South or Bengali in the East.

Writing was introduced relatively late to India, and it did not immediately become important since oral learning was the primary means of transmitting knowledge. Rhys Davids suggests that writing may have been introduced from the Middle East by traders, but Sanskrit, which had been used exclusively in sacred contexts, remained a purely oral language until well into India's classical age. It is interesting to note the importance that Sanskrit orthography and Vedic philosophy of sound play in Hindu symbolism, as the *Varnamala*, or sound-garland/alphabet, of 51 letters is also seen to be represented by the 51 skulls of Kali. In the Upanishads, the transcendent-immanent nature of *Brahman* is represented by the half-matra, or sphota of sound that is inherent to a beat of sound in the Sanskrit system, as one cannot conceptualize it but realizes it is the inherent base of all else.

Transliteration: There are many transliteration schemes for writing Sanskrit using Latin script. Most commonly used are IAST (International Alphabet of Sanskrit Transliteration), which is the academic standard and includes diacritical marks. Other transcription schemes have evolved due to difficulties representing Sanskrit characters in computer systems. These include Harvard-Kyoto that was used earlier, and ITRANS, a lossless transliteration scheme that is used widely on the Internet. For scholarly work, Devanagari has generally been preferred for the transcription and reproduction of whole texts and lengthy excerpts; however, references to individual words and names in texts composed in European languages are usually represented using Roman transliteration.

MORPHOLOGY AND SYNTAX

Classification of verbs: Sanskrit has ten classes of verbs divided into in two broad groups: athematic and thematic. The thematic verbs are so called because an a, called the theme vowel, is inserted between the stem and the ending. This serves to make the thematic verbs generally more well-behaved. Exponents utilized in verb conjugation include prefixes, suffixes, infixes, and reduplication. Also extremely common is vowel gradation; every root has (not necessarily all distinct) zero, guna, and vrdhii grades. If V is the vowel of the zero grade, the guna grade vowel is traditionally thought of a V + a, and the vrdhii grade vowel as V + aa.

Conjugation of verbs: The verbs tenses (a very inexact application of the word, since more distinctions than simply tense are expressed) are organized into four 'systems' (plus gerunds and infinitives, along with such creatures as intensives/frequentives, desideratives, causatives, and benedictives derived from more basic forms). Each verb is also has a grammatical voice: either active, passive or middle. There is also an impersonal voice which can be described as the passive voice of intransitive verbs. The four kinds of tenses are:

PRESENT (PRESENT, IMPERFECT, IMPERATIVE, POTENTIAL)

Nominal Inflection: Sanskrit is a highly inflected language with three grammatical genders (masculine, feminine, neuter) and three numbers (singular, plural, dual). It has eight cases: nominative, vocative, accusative, instrumental, dative, ablative, genitive, and locative. It has over ten noun declensions.

Compounds: One other notable feature of the nominal system is the very common use of nominal compounds, which may be huge (10+ words) like in some modern languages like German language. Nominal compounds occur with various meanings, some examples of which are:

1. *Dvandva (co-ordinative):* These consist of two substantives,

connected in sense with 'and', e.g. matara-pitara 'Mother and Father'.

2. *Bahuvrihi (possessive):* Bahuvrihi, or much-rice, denotes a rich person—one who has much rice. Bahuvrihi compounds refer to a thing which is not specified in any of the parts of which the compound is formed (in other words, they are adjectives). A block-head, for example, is someone whose head is said to be as thick as a block.
3. *Tatpurusha (determinative):* There are many tatpurushas (one for each of the nominal cases, and a few others besides); in a tatpurusha, one component is related to another. For example, a doghouse is a dative compound, a house for a dog. It would be called a "caturtitatpurusha" (caturti refers to the fourth case—that is, the dative). Incidentally, "tatpurusha" is a tatpurusha ("this man"—meaning someone's agent), while "caturtitatpurusha" is a karmadhariya, being both dative, and a tatpurusha.
4. *Karmadharaya (descriptive):* The relation of the first member to the last is appositional, attributive or adverbial, e.g. uluka-yatu (owl+demon) is a demon in the shape of an owl.
5. *Amredita (iterative):* Repetition of a word expresses repetitiveness, e.g. dive-dive 'day by day', 'daily'.

Influences

Modern Day India: Sanskrit's greatest influence, presumably, is that it exerted on languages that grew from its vocabulary and grammatical base. Especially among elite circles in India, Sanskrit is prized as a storehouse of scripture and the language of prayers in Hinduism. While vernacular prayer is common, Sanskrit Mantras are recited by millions of Hindus and most temple functions are conducted entirely in Sanskrit, often Vedic in form.

Most higher forms of Indian vernacular languages like Bengali, Gujarati, and Hindi, often called *Suddha* (pure, higher) are much more heavily Sanskritized. Of modern day Indian languages, while Hindi and Urdu tends to be, in spoken form, more heavily weighted with Persian influence, Bengali and Marathi still retain a largely Sanskrit vocabulary base.

The national anthem, *Jana Gana Mana* and the national song, *Vande Mataram* are both higher forms of Bengali, so Sanskritized as to be archaic in modern usages. But as a medium of instruction for Hindus in India, Sanskrit is still prized and widespread within the educated echelons of society. Sanskrit words are found in many other present-day non-Indian languages. For instance, the Thai language contains many loan words from Sanskrit, and ranged as far as the Philippines viz. Tagalog 'guru', or 'teacher', with the Hindu seafarers who traded there.

Interactions with Sino-Tibetan Languages: Sanskrit and related languages have also influenced their Sino-Tibetan-speaking neighbours to the north through the spread of Buddhist texts in translation. Buddhism was spread to China by *Mahyanist* missionaries mostly through translations of *Buddhist Hybrid Sanskrit* and classical Sanskrit texts, and many terms were transliterated directly and added to the Chinese vocabulary. (While Buddhist Hybrid Sanskrit is not Sanskrit, properly speaking, its vocabulary is substantially the same, both because of genetic relationship, and because of conscious imitation on the part of composers. Buddhist texts composed in Sanskrit proper were primarily found in philosophical schools like the *Madhyamaka*.)

Attempts at Revival: Of late, there have been attempts to revive the speaking of this ancient tongue among people of Haryana and other parts of India, so that vast literature available in Sanskrit can be made easily available to everyone. The CBSE (Central Board of Secondary Education) in India has made Sanskrit a third language in the schools it governs. In such schools, learning Sanskrit is compulsory for grades 5 to 8. An option between Sanskrit and Hindi exists for grades 9 and 10.

Many organizations like the Samskrta Bharati are conducting Speak Sanskrit workshops to popularize the language. About four million people are claimed to have acquired the ability to speak Sanskrit.

LITERATURE AND RELIGION

Vedic or Hindu literature consists primarily of the Vedas; but also includes Shruti and various Smriti texts. The Vedic rites were meant to help the participant transform; this was primarily accomplished via sacrifices (such as the agnihotra).

Astronomical references in the Vedas help provide some broad approximations that help date the beginning of the tradition. Due to the precession of the equinoxes, the seasons shift with relation to the fixed zodiac at a rate of about a month every two thousand years. Some Vedic notices mark the beginning of the year at the vernal equinox in Orion; this was the case around 4500 BC.

The rishis saw the universe as going through unceasing change in a cycle of birth and death, free and yet, paradoxically, governed by order. This order was reflected in the bandhu (connections) between the planets, the elements of the body, and the mind. At the deepest level, the whole universe was bound to, and reflected in, the individual consciousness.

The place of sacrifice represents the cosmos. The three fires used stand for the three divisions of space. The course of the sacrifice represents the year, and all such ritual forms part of continuing annual performances. The rite culminates in the ritual rebirth of the yajamana (sacrificer), which signifies the regeneration of his universe. It is sacred theatre, built upon paradoxes of reality, where symbolic deaths of animals and humans, including the yajamana himself, may be enacted.

The Vedic gods represent the cognitive centres of the self. Vedic science is the science of consciousness. These have evolved into the Hindu paths of Yoga and Vedanta, which is a religious path that is the 'essence' of the Vedas.

The Vedic pantheon is considered to consist of thirty-three different gods, which are placed, in groups of eleven, into one of the three different categories: atmospheric, terrestrial, or celestial, each of which has its own area of responsibility. But just because a god is in one category does not mean that it is completely different from a god from another category; for sometimes a god from one category will have some of the same qualities of a god from another category. This is because the Vedic system is recursive. It has developed into a broader group but it is also seen in Vedic philosophy that they are manifestations of one divine ground known as Brahman. This thought of unity is expressed severally in Vedic texts.

The categories of the gods are: (1) Agni, terrestrial; (2) Indra, atmospheric; and (3) Surya or Vishnu, celestial that mirrors the body, prana, and atman division of the individual. Since one aspires to reach the inner being through the prana (atmosphere), many Vedic hymns extol Indra.

The Vedic or Hindu religion presents a unitary view of the universe with God seen as immanent and transcendent in the forms of Ishvara and Brahman, respectively. Brahman is projected into various deities in the human mind. The main deities were Indra, Varuna, Surya (the Sun), Mitra, Vayu, Agni and Soma. Goddesses included Prithvi, Aditi, Ushas and Saraswati. Deities were not viewed as all-powerful. The relationship between the devotee and the deity was one of transaction. Each deity had a specific role; at any given point, a particular deity was considered superior to the others.

The mode of worship was performance of sacrifices and chanting of verses. The priests helped the common man in performing rituals. People prayed for abundance of children, cattle and wealth.

Later Vedic period: The transition from the early to the later Vedic period was marked by the emergence of agriculture as the dominant economic activity and a corresponding decline in the significance of cattle rearing. Several changes went hand in hand with this. For instance, several large kingdoms arose because of the increasing importance of land and its protection.

Kingdoms: Several small kingdoms merged to form a few large ones which were often at war with each other. 16 mahajanapadas (great kingdoms) are referred to in some of the literature. By this time the Aryan tribes had spread from their original home in the west to much of the east and the south. The power of the king greatly increased. Rulers gave themselves titles like ekarat (the one ruler), sarvabhumi (ruler of all the earth) and chakravartin (protector of land). Note that in early Vedic times he was called gopa, protector of cows. The kings performed sacrifices like rajasuya, (royal consecration) vajapeya (drink of strength) and ashvamedha (horse sacrifice). The coronation ceremony was a major social occasion. Several functionaries came into being in addition to the purohita and the senani of earlier times. The participation of the people in the activities of the government decreased.

Society: The concept of Varna and the rules of marriage became rigid, but not yet watertight. The status of the Brahmanas and Kshatriyas increased greatly. To legitimize their position and the increase their power, the Brahmanas proliferated a large number of sacrifices, developed extreme specialization, and also restricted social mobility. The proper enunciation of verses was considered essential for prosperity and success in war. Kshatriyas amassed wealth, and commissioned the performance of sacrifices. Many rituals emerged to strengthen the alliance between these two groups. But the Varna system in India has remained fluid.

5

Geography and Flora & Fauna

GEOGRAPHY

Haryana is a landlocked state in northern India. It is between 27°39' to 30°35' N latitude and between 74°28' and 77°36' E longitude. The total geographical area of the state is 4.42 m ha, which is 1.4% of the geographical area of the country. The altitude of Haryana varies between 700 and 3600 ft (200 metres to 1200 metres) above sea level.Haryana has only 4% (compared to national 21.85%) area under forests.

Geography of Haryana is a small state in north India. It has a total of 81 cities and towns. It has 6, 759 villages. For administrative purpose the state is divided into four divisions - Ambala, Rohtak, Gurgaon and Hissar.

There are 19 districts, 47 subdivisions, 67 tehsils, 45 sub-tehsils and 116 blocks. Haryana is situated in the north between 27 deg 37' to 30 deg 35' latitude and between 74 deg 28' to 77 deg 36' longitude. Haryana has Uttar Pradesh (UP) on its eastern border, Punjab on its western border, Uttaranchal, Himachal Pradesh & Shivalik Hills on its northern border and Delhi, Rajasthan and Aravali Hills on its southern border.

The altitude of Haryana varies between 700 ft to 900 ft above the sea level. An area of 1, 553 sq. km is covered by forest.

Haryana has four main geographical features.

1. *Shivalik Hills:* Altitude varying between 900 to 2300 meters. These hills are the source of the rivers like Saraswati, Ghaggar, Tangri and Markanda. Parts of Panchkula, Ambala and Yamunanagar districts.
2. *Ghaggar Yamuna Plain:* Divided in 2 parts - the higher one is called 'Bangar' and the lower 'Khadar'. This alluvium plain is made up of sand, clay, silt and hard calcareous balls like gravel known locally as kankar.
3. *Semi-desert Sandy Plain:* This area includes the districts of Sirsa and parts of Hissar, Mahendergarh, Fatehabad, Bhiwani and shares border with Rajasthan.
4. *Aravali Hills:* This is a dry irregular hilly area. Area of Haryana: 44, 212 sq. km

***Population:* 2, 10, 83, 000** (2001 Census)

Climate of Haryana is similar to other states of India lying in the northern plains. It is very hot in summer (up to a high of 50 deg Celsius) and cold in winters (down to a low of 1 deg Celsius). The hottest months are May and June and the coldest being December and January. Rainfall is varied, with Shivalik Hills region being the wettest and the Aravali Hills region being the driest. About 80% of the rainfall occurs in the monsoon season (July-September) and sometimes causes local flooding.

Rivers of Haryana: The river Yamuna flows along its eastern boundary. The ancient Saraswati river was thought to have flowed throw Haryana but it has now disappeared. The river Ghaggar is its main seasonal river.

It rises up in the outer Himalayas between the Yamuna and the Sutluj and enters Haryana near Pinjore, district Panchkula. Passing through Ambala and Hissar it reaches Bikaner in Rajasthan and runs a course of 290 miles before disappearing in the deserts of Rajasthan. The Markanda river's ancient name was Aruna. A seasonal stream like the Ghaggar, it originates from the lower Shivalik hills and enters Haryana near Ambala.

During monsoons, this stream swells up into a raging torrent notorious for its devastating power. The surplus water is carried on to the Sanisa lake where the Markanda joins the Saraswati. An important tributary is the Tangri. The Sahibi originates in the Mewat hills near Jitgarh and Manoharpur in Rajasthan. Gathering volume from about a hundred tributaries, it reaches voluminous proportions, forming a broad stream around Alwar and Patan.

On reaching Rohtak its branches off into two smaller streams, finally reaching the outskirts of Delhi and flowing into the Yamuna. There are three other rivulets in and around the Mewat hills – Indori, Dohan and Kasavati and they all flow northwards from the south.

Transport System: The main transport systems in Haryana are Roads and Railway.

Roads: Haryana has a total length of 29, 524 kilometres of paved (metalled) roads; making it one of the most well connected states in whole of Asia. Every village of the state is now linked with paved roads.

The state government proposes to construct Express highway and free ways for speedier vehicular traffic. Government encourages private sector investment in this sector for up gradation of roads, construction of ROB and BOT basis including four lane ROB. The length of the national highways passing through Haryana is 665 km. The following five national highways pass through Haryana. 1. National Highway 1 (NH1) Delhi- Karnal - Kurukshetra - Ambala - Amritsar. Famous as the GT Road. 2. National Highway 10 (NH10) Delhi - Rohtak- Hansi - Hissar - Fatehabad - Sirsa- Ferozepur. 3. National Highway 21 (NH21) Chandigarh - Panchkula - Pinjore- Kalka - Shimla. 4. National Highway 2 (NH2) Delhi- Faridabad - Mathura - Agra - Mumbai (Bombay) 5. National Highway 8 (NH8) Delhi - Gurgaon - Jaipur - Mumbai (Bombay).

Details of Highways and Roads: National Highways: 656 km State Highways: 3135 km District roads: 1587 km

Rural and other roads: 17190 km.

Haryana Roadways: The total number of buses plied by Haryana Roadways is 3, 411. There are a total of 82 Bus Stands and 20 Bus Depots. About 10, 75, 000 passengers travel by these buses everyday. Haryana was the first state in India to introduce luxury video coaches.

Railway System: Haryana is well connected on the rail network. Under the National Capital Region (NCR) scheme there is already a proposal to provide rail corridor connecting towns around Delhi linking the major satellite towns like Faridabad, Gurgaon, Kundli, Bahadurgarh etc. Similarly, there is also a proposal to provide rapid mass transportation system between Delhi and these satellite towns. The main railway routes passing through Haryana are: Amritsar - Delhi Rewari - Ahemdabad Bhiwani - Rohtak-Delhi Ambala- Ferozepur Delhi - Ferozepur Kalka - Jodhpur Kalka - Howrah Amritsar - Howrah Delhi

Shimla Water: All the 6, 759 villages of Haryana are now provided with safe drinking water facilities. In addition there are 68 partial urban water supply schemes. Water is available as Haryana is a land of canals. It has tapped its ground water resources to maximum.

Life irrigation schemes, pump sets, and water channels supply adequate amount of water to the fields and industries. The State has already launched an ambitious program of brick lining the water courses. The Sutluj-Yamuna Link canal (SYL) will further add to Haryana's prosperity.

Haryana is a landlocked state in northern India. It is located between 27°37' to 30°35' N latitude and between 74°28' and 77°36' E longitude. The altitude of Haryana varies between 700 to 3600 ft. (200 metres to 2 kilometres) above sea level. An area of 1, 553 km^2 is covered by forest. Haryana has four main geographical features.

- The Yamuna-Ghaggar plain forming the largest part of the state

- The Shivalik Hills to the northeast
- Semi-desert sandy plain to the southwest
- The Aravali Range in the south

The majority of the state is an agricultural plain, with the southern and western edge being more dry and arid.

PLAINS AND MOUNTAINS

Haryana has four main geographical features.

- The Yamuna-Ghaggar plain forming the largest part of the state is also called Delhi doab consisting of *Sutlej-Ghaggar doab* (between Sutlej in north in Punjab and Ghaggar riverflowing through northern Haryana), *Ghaggar-Hakra doab* (between Ghaggar river and Hakra or Drishadvati river which is the paleo channel of the holy Sarasvati River) and *Hakra-Yamuna doab* (between Hakra river and Yamuna).
- The Lower Shivalik Hills to the northeast in foothills of Himalaya
- The Bagar tract semi-desert dry sandy plain to the south-west.
- The Aravali Range's northern most low rise isolated non-continuous outcrops in the south

Hydrography

The Yamuna, tributary of Ganges, flows along the state's eastern boundary.

Northern Haryana has several north-east to south-west flowing rivers originating from the Sivalik Hills of Himalayas, such as Ghaggar-Hakra(palaeochannel of vedic Sarasvati river), Chautang (paleochannel of vedic Drishadvati river, tributary of Ghagghar), Tangri river(tributary of Ghagghar), Kaushalya river (tributary of Ghagghar), Markanda River (tributary of Ghagghar), Sarsuti,Dangri, Somb river. Haryana's main seasonal river, the Ghaggar-Hakra, known as Ghaggar before the Ottu barrage and as the Hakra downstream of the barrage, rises in the outer Himalayas, between the Yamuna and the Satluj and enters the state near Pinjore in the Panchkula district, passes through Ambala and Sirsa, it reaches Bikaner in Rajasthan and runs for 460 km (290 mi) before disappearing into the deserts of Rajasthan.

The seasonal Markanda River, known as the *Aruna* in ancient times, originates from the lower Shivalik Hills and enters Haryana west of Ambala, and swells into a raging torrent during monsoon is notorious for its devastating power, carries its surplus water on to the *Sanisa Lake* where the *Markanda* joins the *Sarasuti* and later the *Ghaggar*.

Southern Haryana has several south-east to north-west flowing seasonal rivulets originating from the Aravalli Range in and around the hills in Mewat region, including Sahibi River (called Najafgarh drain in Delhi), Dohan river (tributary of Sahibi, originates at Mandoli village near Neem Ka Thana in Jhunjhunu district of Rajasthan and then disappears in Mahendragarh district), Krishnavati river (former tributary of Sahibi river, originates near Dariba and disappears in Mahendragarh district much before reaching Sahibi river) and Indori river (longest tributary of Sahibi River, originates in Sikar district of Rajasthan and flows to Rewari district of Haryana), these once were tributaries of the Drishadwati/Saraswati river.

Major canals are Western Yamuna Canal, Sutlej Yamuna link canal (from Sutlej river tributary of Indus), and Indira Gandhi Canal.

Major dams are Kaushalya Dam in Panchkula district, Hathnikund Barrage and Tajewala Barrage on Yamuna in Yamunanagar district, Pathrala barrage on Somb river in Yamunanagar district, ancient Anagpur Dam near Surajkund in Faridabad district, and Ottu barrage on Ghaggar-Hakra River in Sirsa district.

Major lakes are Dighal Wetland, Basai Wetland, Badkhal Lake in Faridabad, holy Brahma Sarovar and Sannihit Sarovar in Kurukshetra, Blue Bird Lake in Hisar, Damdama Lake at Sohna in Gurgram district, Hathni Kund in Yamunanagar district, Karna Lake at Karnal, ancient Surajkund in Faridabad, and Tilyar Lake in Rohtak.

The *Haryana State Waterbody Management Board* is responsible for rejuvenation of 14,000 Johads of Haryana and up to 60 lakes in National Capital Region falling within the Haryana state.

Only hot spring of Haryana is the Sohna Sulphur Hot Spring at Sohna in Gurugram district. Tosham Hill range has several sacred sulphur pond of religious significance that are revered for the healing impact of sulfur, such as *Pandu Teerth Kund, Surya Kund, Kukkar Kund, Gyarasia Kund* or *Vyas Kund.*

Seasonal waterfalls include Tikkar Taal twin lakes at Morni hiills, Dhosi Hill in Mahendragarh district and Pali village on outskirts of Faridabad.

Climate

Haryana is extremely hot in summer at around 45 °C (113 °F) and mild in winter.

The hottest months are May and June and the coldest December and January. The climate is arid to semi-arid with average rainfall of 354.5 mm. Around 29% of rainfall is received during the months from July to September, and the remaining rainfall is received during the period from December to February.

FLORA AND FAUNA

Forests

Forest Cover in the state in 2013 was 3.59% (1586 km) and the Tree Cover in the state was 2.90% (1282 km), giving a total forest and tree Cover of 6.49%. In 2016-17, 18,412 hectares were brought under tree cover by planting 14.1 million seedlings.

Thorny, dry, deciduous forest and thorny shrubs can be found all over the state. During the monsoon, a carpet of grass covers the hills.

Mulberry, eucalyptus, pine, kikar, shisham and babul are some of the trees found here. The species of fauna found in the state of Haryana include black buck, nilgai, panther, fox, mongoose, jackal and wild dog. More than 450 species of birds are found here.

Wildlife

Haryana has two national parks, eight wildlife sanctuaries, two wildlife conservation areas, four animal and bird breeding centers, one deer park and three zoos, all of which are managed by the Haryana Forest Department of the Government of Haryana.

Environmental and ecological issues

Haryana Environment Protection Council is the advisory committee and | Department of Environment, Haryana]] is the department responsible for administration of environment. Areas of Haryana surrounding Delhi NCR are most polluted. During smog of November 2017, Air quality index of Gurugram and Faridabad showed that the density of Fine particulates (2.5 PM diameter) was an average of 400 PM and monthly average of Haryana was 60 PM. Other sources of pollution are exhaust gases from old vehicles, stone crushers and brick kiln. Haryana has 75 lakh (7,500,000) old vehicles, of which 40% are old more polluting vehicles, besides 500,000 new vehicles are added every year. Other majorly polluted cities are Bhiwani, Bahadurgarh, Dharuhera, Hisar and Yamunanagar.

Flora & Fauna In Haryana

At one time Haryana was a forest covered land, but today only about 3.5 per cent of the total area is remains so.

A thorny dry deciduous forest, pine and thorny shrubs can be found all over the state. Chief trees are mulberry, eucalyptus, pine, kikar, sheesham and babul, and during the monsoon a carpet of grass covers the hills which makes them excellent grazing ground for black buck and nilgai (blue bull).

A lone tiger or panther can be spotted on occasion, while foxes, mongooses, jackals and wild dogs are aplenty.

6

Economy

INTRODUCTION

Haryana's 14th placed 12.96% 2012-17 CAGR estimated 2017-18 GSDP of US$95 billion is split in to 52% services, 30% industries and 18% agriculture.

Services sector is split across 45% in real estate and financial & professional services, 26% trade and hospitality, 15% state and central govt employees, and 14% transport and logistics & warehousing. In IT services, Gurugram ranks number 1 in India in growth rate and existing technology infrastructure, and number 2 in startup ecosystem, innovation and livability (Nov 2016).

Industries sector is split across 69% manufacturing, 28% construction, 2% utilities and 1% mining. In industrial manufacturing, Haryana produces India's 67% of passenger cars, 60% of motorcycles, 50% of tractors and 50% of the refrigerators.

Services and industrial sectors are boosted by 7 operational SEZs and additional 23 formally approved SEZs (20 already notified and 3 in-principal approval) that are mostly spread along the Delhi–Mumbai Industrial Corridor, Amritsar Delhi Kolkata Industrial Corridor and Delhi Western Peripheral Expressway in NCR).

Agriculture sector is split across 93% crops and livestock, 4% commercial forestry and logging, and 2% fisheries. Agriculture sector of Haryana, with only less than 1.4% area of India, contributes 15% food grains to the central food security public distribution system, and 7% of total national agricultural exports including 60% of total national Basmati rice export.

Agriculture

Crops

Haryana is traditionally an agrarian society of zamindars (owner-cultivator farmers). The Green Revolution in Haryana of 1960s combined with completion of Bhakra Dam in 1963 and Western Yamuna Command Network canal system in 1970s resulted in the significantly increased food grain production.

In 2015-2016, Haryana produced the following principal crops: 13,352,000 tonne wheat, 4,145,000 tonne rice, 7,169,000 tonne sugarcane, 993,000 tonne cotton and 855,000 tonne oilseeds (mustard seed, sunflower, etc.).

Fruits, vegetables and spices

Vegetable production was: Potato 853,806 tonnes, Onion 705,795 tonnes, Tomato 675,384 tonnes, Cauliflower 578,953 tonnes, Leafy Vegetables 370,646 tonnes, Brinjal 331,169 tonnes, guard 307,793 tonnes, Peas 111,081 tonnes and others 269,993 tonnes.

Fruits production was: Citrus 301,764 tonnes, Guava 152,184 tonnes, Mango 89,965 tonnes, Chikoo 16,022 tonnes, Aonla 12,056 tonnes and other fruits 25,848 tonnes.

Spices production was: Garlic 40,497 tonnes, Fenugreek 9,348 tonnes, Ginger 4,304 tonnes and others 840 tonnes.

Flowers and medicinal plants

Cut flowers production was: Marigold 61,830 tonnes, Gladiolus 24,486,200 lakh, Rose 18,611,600 lakh and other 6,913,000 lakh.

Medicinal plants production was: Aloe vera 1403 tonnes and Stevia 13 tonnes.

Livestock

Haryana is well known for its high-yield Murrah buffalo. Other breeds of cattle native to Haryana are Haryanvi, Mewati, Sahiwal and Nili-Ravi.

Research

To support its agrarian economy, both central government (Central Institute for Research on Buffaloes, Central Sheep Breeding Farm, National Research Centre on Equines, Central Institute of Fisheries, National Dairy Research Institute, Indian Institute of Wheat and Barley Research and National Bureau of Animal Genetic Resources) and state government (CCS HAU, LUVAS, Government Livestock Farm, Regional Fodder Station and Northern Region Farm Machinery Training and Testing Institute) have opened several institutes for research and education.

MACRO-ECONOMY OF HARYANA

As per Sept 2017 data, Haryana state's GSDP was US$85 billion in 2016-17 (estimated to be US$95 billion in 2017-2018, comparable to Angola), which had grown at 12.96% CAGR between 2012-17, boosted by the fact that this state on DMIC in NCR contributes 7% of India's agricultural exports and 60% of India's Basmati rice export, with 7 operational SEZs and additional 23 formally approved SEZs (20 already notified and 3 in-principal approval, mostly along Delhi Western Peripheral Expressway as well as Amritsar Delhi Kolkata Industrial Corridor and DMIC corridor) also produces India's 67% of passenger cars, 60% of motorcycles, 50% of tractors and 50% of the refrigerators, which places Haryana on 14th place on the list of Indian states and union territories by GDP behind only much bigger states that are significantly larger in both area and population.As per Nov 2016 data, Gurugram ranks number

1 in India in IT growth rate and existing technology infrastructure, and number 2 in startup ecosystem, innovation and livability.

Macro-economic trend

This is a chart of trend of gross state domestic product of Haryana at market prices estimated by *Ministry of Statistics and Programme Implementation* with figures in CroreRupees.

Year	Gross State Domestic Product
1999–2000	50,787
2000–2001	56,955
2001–2002	63,489
2002–2003	69,653
2003–2004	78,816
2004–2005	89,431
2005–2006	100,676
2007–2008	101,319.42

Sectors

Digital economy

BharatNet roll out is already complete in Haryana by November 2017 by providing impetus to Make in India and Digital India. Gurugram is among India's top 3 IT hubs and IT export income earner.

Manufacturing

There are numerous manufacturing companies in the region. These include Hindustan National Glass, Maruti Udyog Limited, Escorts Group, Hero MotoCorp, Alcatel, Sony, Whirlpool India, Bharti Telecom, Liberty Shoes and HMT. In addition there are more than 80,000 small-scale industrial units in the state which cumulatively bring in a substantial income for the state and its people. Yamunanagar district has a paper mill BILT, Haryana has a large production of cars, motorcycles, tractors, sanitary ware, glass container industry, gas stoves and scientific instruments.

Faridabad is another big industrial part of Haryana. It is home to hundreds of large scale companies like Orient fans (C.K.Birla Group), JCB India Limited, Nirigemes, Agri Machinery Group (Escorts Group), Yamaha Motor India Pvt. Ltd., Whirlpool, ABB, Goodyear Tire and Rubber Company, Knorr Bremse India Pvt. Ltd. There are thousands of medium and small scale units as well, like Amrit Enterprises, McAma Industries.

Agriculture

About 86% of the area is arable, and of that 96% is cultivated. About 75% of the area is irrigated, through tubewells and an extensive system of canals. Haryana contributed significantly to the Green Revolution in India in the 1970s that made the country self-sufficient in food production. The state has also significantly contributed to the field of agricultural education in the country. Haryana's agriculture GDP contribution to the nation's agricultural GDP is 14.1% and HAU Hisar in Haryana is Asia's largest agricultural university. In 2017-18, out of total 1,350 canal tails, 1343 tails have been fully fed.

Dairy farming

Dairy farming is also an essential part of the rural economy. Haryana has a livestock population of 10 million head. Milk and milk products form an essential part of the local diet. There is a saying *Desaan main des Haryana, jit doodh dahi ka khaana,* which means "Best among all the countries in the world is Haryana, where the staple food is milk and yogurt". Haryana, with 660 grams of availability of milk per capita per day, ranks at number two in the country compared to the national average of 232 grams. There is a vast network of milk societies that support the dairy industry. The National Dairy Research Institute at Karnal, and the Central Institute for Research on Buffaloes at Hisar are instrumental in development of new breeds of cattle and propagation of these breeds through embryo transfer technology.

Roads, aviation and infrastructure

Haryana has a total road length of 23,684 kilometers. The most remote parts of the state are linked with metaled roads. Its modern bus fleet of 3,864 buses covers a distance of 1.15 million Kilometers per day. It was the first State in the country to introduce luxury video coaches.

Haryana State has always given high priority to the expansion of electricity infrastructure, as it is one of the most important inputs for the development of the State. Haryana was the first State in the country to achieve 100% rural electrification in 1970, first in the country to link all villages with all weather roads and first in the country to provide safe drinking water facilities throughout the state.

AGRICULTURE

Despite recent industrial development, Haryana is primarily an agricultural state. About 70% of residents are engaged in agriculture. Wheat and rice are the major crops. Haryana is self-sufficient in food production and the second largest contributor to India's central pool of food grains. Other crops include sugarcane, cotton, maize, bajra, and oilseeds. About 86% of the area is arable, and of that 96% is cultivated. About 75% of the area is irrigated, through tubewells and an extensive system of canals. Haryana contributed significantly to the Green Revolution in India in the 1970s that made the country self-sufficient in food production.

Dairy farming is also an essential part of the rural economy. Milk and milk products form an essential part of the local diet. There is the saying *Desaan main des Haryana, jit doodh dahi ka khaana*, which means "Among places is Haryana, where the staple food is milk and yoghurt". There is a vast network of milk societies that support the dairy industry. The National Dairy Research Institute at Karnal, and the Central Institute for Research on Buffaloes at Hisar are instrumental in development of new breeds of cattle and propagation of these breeds through embryo transfer technology. The Murrah breed of water buffalo from Haryana is world-famous for its milk production.

MANUFACTURING

More than a thousand medium and large industries with a capital investment of Rs. 200 billion or $ 4.4 billion have been established in the state in mainly Gurgaon, Panchkula and Faridabad. These include Maruti Udyog Limited, Escorts, Hero Honda, Alcatel, Sony , Whirlpool India , Bharti Telecom, Liberty Shoes and Hindustan Machine Tools. In addition there are more than 80, 000 small-scale industries in the state which cumulatively bring in a substantial income for the state and its people. Yamunanagar district has a BILT paper mill, Haryana has a large production of cars, motorcycles, tractors, sanitary ware, gas stoves and scientific instruments.

MACROECONOMIC TREND

This is a chart of trend of gross state domestic product of Haryana at market prices estimated by *Ministry of Statistics and Programme Implementation* with figures in millions of Indian Rupees.

Year	*Gross State Domestic Product*
1980	33, 860
1985	65, 520
1990	136, 360
1995	297, 890
2000	550, 050

Haryana's gross state domestic product for 2004 is estimated at $25 billion at current prices.

Over 3% of the *S&P CNX 500* conglomerates have corporate

offices in Haryana.

SERVICE INDUSTRY

Gurgaon has seen emergence of an active information technology industry in the recent years. With organisations like IBM, Hewitt Associates, Dell, Convergys, United Healthcare and NIIT setting up back offices or contact centres in Gurgaon.

INDUSTRIAL SECTOR

Manufacturing

The headquarters of DLF Limited, India's largest real estate company, in Gurgaon, Haryana.

- Faridabad is one of the biggest industrial city of Haryana as well as North India. The City is home to large-scale MNC companies like India Yamaha Motor Pvt. Ltd., Havells India Limited, JCB India Limited, Indian Oil (R&D), and Larsen & Toubro (L&T).Eyewear e-tailer Lenskart and healthcare startup Lybrate have their headquarters in Faridabad.
- Hissar, a NCR Counter Magnet city known as steel and cotton spinning hub as well as upcoming integrated industrial aerocity and aero MRO hub at Hisar Airport, is a fast developing city and the hometown of Navin Jindal and Subhash Chandra of Zee TV fame. Savitri Jindal, Navin Jindal's mother, has been listed by *Forbes* as the third richest woman in world.
- Panipat has heavy industry, including a refinery operated by the Indian Oil Corporation, a urea manufacturing plant operated by National Fertilizers Limited and a National Thermal Power Corporation power plant. It is known for its woven *modhas* or round stools.
- Sonepat: IMT Kundli, Nathupur, Rai and Bari are industrial areas with several Small and medium-sized enterprises, including come large ones such as Atlas cycles, E.C.E., Birla factory, OSRAM
- Gurugram: IMT Minesar, Dundahera and Sohna are industrial and logistics hub, that also has National Security Guards, Indian Institute of Corporate Affairs, National Brain Research Centre and National Bomb Data Centre.

Utilities

Haryana State has always given high priority to the expansion of electricity infrastructure, as it is one of the most important inputs for the development of the state. Haryana was the first state in the country to achieve 100% rural electrification in 1970 as well as the first in the country to link all villages with all-weather roads and provide safe drinking water facilities throughout the state.

Power in the state are:

1. Renewable and non-polluting sources

(a) Hydroelectricity

- Bhakra-Nangal Dam Hydroelectric Power Plant
- WYC Hydro Electric Station, 62.4 MW, Yamunanagar

(b) Solar power stations

- Faridabad Solar Power Plant: being setup by HPGCL Faridabad (c.2016).

2. Nuclear power stations

(a) Gorakhpur Nuclear Power Plant, 2800MW, Fatehabad, Phase-I 1400MW by 2021

3. Coal-fired thermal power stations

(a) Deenbandhu Chhotu Ram Thermal Power Station, 600MW, Yamunanagar,

(b) Indira Gandhi Super Thermal Power Project, 1500MW, Jhajjar

(c) Jhajjar Power Station, 1500MW

(d) Panipat Thermal Power Station I, 440MW

(e) Panipat Thermal Power Station II, 920MW

(f) Rajiv Gandhi Thermal Power Station, 1200MW, Hisar

SERVICES SECTOR

Transport

Roads and Highways

Haryana has a total road length of 26,062 kilometres (16,194 mi), including 2,482 kilometres (1,542 mi) 29 national highways, 1,801 kilometres (1,119 mi) state highways, 1,395 kilometres (867 mi) Major District Roads (MDR) and 20,344 kilometres (12,641 mi) Other District Roads (ODR) (c. December 2017). A fleet of 3,864 Haryana Roadways buses covers a distance of 1.15 million km per day, and it was the first state in the country to introduce luxury video coaches.

Ancient Delhi Multan Road and Grand Trunk Road, South Asia's oldest and longest major roads, pass through Haryana. GT Road passes through the districts of Sonipat, Panipat, Karnal, Kurukshetra and Ambala in north Haryana where it enters Delhi and subsequently the industrial town of Faridabad on its way.

The 135.6 kilometres (84.3 mi) Kundli-Manesar-Palwal Expressway(KMP) will provide a high-speed link to northern Haryana with its southern districts such as Sonepat, Gurgaon, Jhajjar and Faridabad.

The Delhi-Agra Expressway (NH-2) that passes through Faridabad is being widened to six lanes from current four lanes. It will further boost Faridabad's connectivity with Delhi.

Railway

Rail network in Haryana is covered by 5 rail divisions under 3 rail zones. Diamond Quadrilateral High-speed rail network, Eastern Dedicated Freight Corridor (72 km) and Western Dedicated Freight Corridor (177 km) pass through Haryana.

Bikaner railway division of North Western Railway zone manages rail network in western and southern Haryana covering Bhatinda-Dabwali-Hanumangarh line, Rewari-Bhiwani-Hisar-Bathinda line, Hisar-Sadulpur line and Rewari-Loharu-Sadulpur line.

Jaipur railway division of North Western Railway zone manages rail network in south-west Haryana covering Rewari-Reengas-Jaipur line, Delhi-Alwar-Jaipur line and Loharu-Sikar line.

Delhi railway division of Northern Railway zone manages rail network in north and east and central Haryana covering Delhi-Ambala line, Delhi-Rohtak-Tohana line, Rewari–Rohtak line, Jind-Sonepat line and Delhi-Rewari line. Agra railway division of North Central Railway zone manages another very small part of network in south-east Haryana covering Palwal-Mathura line only.

Ambala railway division of Northern Railway zone manages small part of rail network in north-east Haryana covering Ambala-Yamunanagar line, Ambala-Kurukshetra line and UNESCO World Heritage Kalka–Shimla Railway.

Metro

Delhi Metro connects the national capital Delhi with NCR cities such as Faridabad, Gurugram and Bahadurgarh. Faridabad has the longest metro network in the NCR Region consisting of 9 stations and track length being 14 km.

Sky Way

The Haryana and Delhi governments have constructed the 4.5-kilometre (2.8 mi) international standard Delhi Faridabad Skyway, the first of its kind in North India, to connect Delhi and Faridabad.

Communication and media

Haryana has a statewide network of telecommunication facilities.

Haryana Government has its own statewide area network by which all government offices of 22 districts and 126 blocks across the state are connected with each other thus making it the first SWAN of the country.

Bharat Sanchar Nigam Limited and most of the leading private sector players (such as Reliance Infocom, Tata Teleservices, Bharti Telecom, Idea Vodafone Essar, Aircel, Uninor and Videocon) have operations in the state. Two biggest cities of Haryana, Faridabad and Gurgaon which are part of National Capital Region come under the local Delhi Mobile Telecommunication System.

The rest of the cities of Haryana comes under Haryana Telecommunication System.

Electronic media channels include, MTV, 9XM, Star Group, SET Max, News Time, NDTV 24x7 and Zee Group. The radio stations include All India Radio and other FM stations.

The major newspapers of Haryana include *Dainik Bhaskar*, *Punjab Kesari*, *Jag Bani*, *Dainik Jagran*, *The Tribune*, *Amar Ujala*, *Hindustan Times*, *Dainik Tribune*, *The Times of India*and *Hari-Bhumi*.

Healthcare

The Total Fertility Rate of Haryana is 2.3. The Infant Mortality Rate is 41 (SRS 2013) and Maternal Mortality Ratio is 146 (SRS 2010–2012).

7

Tourism

Tourism in Haryana relates to tourism in the state of Haryana, India. There are 21 tourism hubs created by Haryana Tourism, which are located in Ambala, Bhiwani Faridabad, Fatehabad, Gurgaon, Hisar, Jhajjar, Jind, Kaithal, Karnal, Kurukshetra, Panchkula, Sirsa, Sonipat, Panipat, Rewari, Rohtak, Yamunanagar, Palwal and Mahendergarh.

Haryana is officially part of Mahabharata and Krishna tourism development circuit plans of government of India and government of Haryana.

Gurgaon

District Gurgaon of Haryana: The district headquarter is situated in Gurgaon city. Other smaller towns are Nuh, Ferozepur Jhirka, Sohna, and Pataudi. Total area of the district is 2,105 sq. km and its population is 11,46,000.

Because of its close proximity to Delhi and excellent infrastructure, Gurgaon has become one of the most important corporate and industrial hubs of India. The corporate office and manufacturing plant of India's largest car maker Maruti Udyog Limited (promoted by Suzuki Motors) is situated here, as are a large number other industries. The main manufacturing unit of Hero Honda is also situated in Gurgaon. Other areas in which Gurgaon is excelling are the Information Technology (IT) industry, Software development and Call Centres.

In Mahabharata times, Gurgaon was a thick forest where the ashram of Guru Dronacharya existed. It was here that Pandav and Kourav princes got their training in arms and warfare. Because of Guru Dronacharya's ashram, people started calling it the 'Gurugram' which later on changed into 'Gurgaon'. This place had been gifted by Yudhister to Guru Dronacharya, as 'guru-dakshina'.

The Sultanpur national park and bird sanctuary as well as the Sohna tourist complex lies in Gurgaon district.

To cater to the corporate clientele, many top class Shopping malls and five star hotels, like The Radisson, have sprung up in Gurgaon. Major information technology (IT) companies like HCL, Hughes Software, TCS, Alcatel, IBM and GE Capital have set their offices at Gurgaon.

Hissar

Hissar District of Haryana: Hissar district, also called Hisar, has an area of 4191 sq. km and its population is 12,30,000. The district headquarter is situated in Hissar city. Hissar is one of the more important districts of Haryana politically. Other smaller towns are Hansi, Uklana, Adampur Agroha and Barwala. Hissar town was one of the prime centres of Harappan culture. The area has been associated with ancient Vedic culture tribes such as Bharatas, Purus, Kurus, Mujavatas and Mahavrishas. During medieval times it went through upheavals and conquests, and gained importance for its strategic location with regard to Delhi.

Feroze Shah Tughluq constructed a fort here and called it Hissar-e-Firoz (fort of Feroze) and dug canals from the Yamuna and Ghaggar rivers to irrigate the dry land. It is a grand structure complete with a basement and a mosque. He built a mosque called Lat ki Masjid. Humayun built a Masjid at Fatehabad, near Hissar town. Emperor Akbar made Hissar the headquarters of the district earlier controlled by Feroze Shah.

During early 19th century the British took Hissar under

their charge along with the rest of Haryana. Hissar is now an important industrial centre of Haryana having lots of Steel and Cotton industries. Chaudhary Charan Singh Agriculture University, also called Hissar Agricultural University is one of the foremost full-fledged educational institutions dedicated solely to agriculture. Beside the above, there are many other monuments like Jahaz kothi, Gujri mahal and Jain pillar.

Ancient Sites: Two sites from the pre-Harappan and Harappan period can be found in Rakhi Garhi and Agroha Mound.

Jhajjar

Jhajjar district, Haryana was carved out of Rohtak district on July 15, 1997. The district headquarter is situated in Jhajjar town at a distance of about 65 km from Delhi. The town is said to have been founded by one Chhaju and Chhajunagar was changed to Jhajjar. It is also derived from Jharnaghar, a natural fountain.

A third derivation is from Jhajjar, a water vessel, because the surface drainage of the country for miles around runs into the town as into a sink. Other towns in the district are Bahadurgarh and Beri. Bahadurgarh was founded by Rathi Jats and formerly known as Sharafabad. It is situated 29 km from Delhi and had developed into an important of industrial canter.

The total area of Jhajjar district is 1,890 sq. km and its population is 7,09,000. The district consists of 2 industrial areas with 2408 plots. The basic industries are ceramics, glass, chemicals, engineering, electrical & electronics. There are 48 large and medium units 213 small scale units with the total investment of Rs. 3400 million ($ 76.5 million) and workforce of 8248. Major crops grown here are Rice, wheat and Maize. The total irrigated agricultural land is about 67,000 hectares.

Jind

The district headquarter is situated in Jind town. Other

smaller towns are Narwana, Safidon and Uchana. The total area of Jind district is 2736 sq. kms and its population is 9,63,000. The town, headquarter of the district of the same name is situated on the Ferozepur-Delhi section of the Northern Railway, 123 kilometres away from Delhi and 57 Kilometres from Rohtak. It is also connected by road with Delhi, Patiala, Chandigarh and other important towns of Haryana.

Jind town has a Arjuna stadium, milk plant, cattle feed plant, Bulbul restaurant and a large grain market. There are facilities for stay at PWD rest house, canal rest house and market committee rest house. The town is well provided with schools, colleges, hospitals and other basic amenities. Jind is noted for its numerous temples sacred to the worship of Shiva. Tradition assigns the settlement of the town to the Mahabharata period.

According to the legend, the Pandavas built here a temple in honour of Jainti Devi (the goddess of victory) and offered prayers for success in their battle against the Kouravas. The town grew up around the temple and was named Jaintapuri, (abode of Jainti Devi) which in course of time corrupted to Jind. Raja Gajpat Singh in 1755 seized a large tract of country including the present districts of Jind from the Afghan and made Jind the capital of the state in 1776. He made a fort here in 1775. Later, Sangrur was chosen as capital of Jind State by Raja Sangat Singh (1822 to 1834 AD).

Kaithal

Kaithal was earlier a part of district Karnal and in 1973 became part of the newly created district of Kurukshetra. Kaithal became a new district of Haryana on 1st November, 1989. The district headquarter is situated in Kaithal town. Other smaller towns are Guhla, Pundri and Cheeka. The total area of Kaithal district is 2,389 sq. km and its population is 8,20,000. Kaithal is known for intensive cultivation of Rice and wheat with a well developed irrigation infrastructure.

Karnal

Karnal, with a population of 8,85,000 covers an area of 1967 sq. km. District headquarter is situated in Karnal city. Karnal was founded by the Kouravs around the time of the Mahabharata for King Karna. It is 123 km from Delhi on the National Highway NH1, (called the GT Road), and 126 km from Chandigarh. Other towns are Gharaunda, Nilokheri, Assandh, Indri and Taraori.

Karnal is famous for Shoes, agriculture research institutions and Basmati Rice.

Karnal, 'city of Daanvir Karan' has been a walled town as far as it is possible to trace and may have had a citadel one time. In 1739, the Persian King Nadir Shah defeated the Mughal ruler Muhammad Shah in the Battle of Karnal. Karnal was annexed by the Raja of Jind in AD 1763 and was taken from him by George Thomas in 1797. The British established a cantonment in 1811, but abandoned it after thirty years due to the outbreak of malaria. Kalpana Chawla the astronaut Brigadier V P Airy, MVC.

Karnal district lies on the western bank of river Yamuna forming the eastern boundary. Yamuna separates Haryana from Uttar Pradesh. The Karnal district including Panipat lies between 29 09'50" and 29 50' North latitude and 76 31' 15" and 77 12'45" East longitude, its height from sea level is around 240 meters. Karnal is surrounded by Kurukshetra district on its northwest, Jind, Kaithal districts on its west, Panipat district on its south and Uttar Pradesh on east.

The district is a part of the Ganga-Saraswati-Indus plains and has a well spread irrigation network of western Yamuna canal. Its geographical area has been divided in to three agro climatic regions, Khadar, Bhangar and Nardak belt. Khadar starts from Indri-Karnal road one mile away from Karnal covering the area in between Yamuna river and National Highway No.1 up to Patti-Kalyana village. Bhangar area starts from west of Khadar area covering Gharaunda, development block. The nardak area lies in Nissing, Nilokheri and Assandh blocks. However, its water is saline and not fit for irrigation.

Karnal is the centre of National Dairy Research Institute (NDRI), CSSRI, Wheat Research Directorate, National Bureau of Animal Genetics Research and Sugarcane Breeding Institute. People can learn flying at the Karnal Flying Club.

Rohtak

Rohtak-District of Haryana: The district headquarter is situated in Rohtak town. Other smaller towns are Hasangarh, Meham, Sampla, and Kalanaur. The total area of Rohtak is 1708 sq. kms and its population is 7,79,000. The Rohtak district is also known as the political capital of Haryana.

'Rohtak' is said to be a corruption of Rohtasgarh, a name applied to the ruined Khokrakot sites of two cities, one lying north of Rohtak and the other about 4 km to the east. It is thought that it was named after Raja Rohtas, in whose days the city was built. It is also claimed that the town derives its name from the Roherra tree called Rohtika in Sanskrit. It is said that the town was build by clearing a forest of Rohtika trees, and hence its name Rohtak.

Another version connects Rohtak with Rohitaka, mentioned in the Mahabharata. It was possibly the capital of Bahudhanyaka. In the Vinaya of Mulasarvasti-vadins, Jivaka is shown as undertaking a journey from Taxila to Bhadramkara, Udumbra, Rohitaka and Mathura in the Ganga Doab.

The ancient road carried the trade of the Ganga valley to Taxila, passing through Rohitaka to Sakala. The ruins of the ancient town are found at Khokrakot or Rohtasgarh. Some experts hold that the town is as old as the Indus Valley Civilization. Some minor finds at Khokrakot are typical of the Indus Valley sites. Clay moulds of coins discovered here have thrown an important light of the process of casting coins in ancient India.

The existence of the town during the rule of the Kushanas is testified by the recent recovery of a Kushana pillar, decorated with carvings of winged lions and riders. An example of a lion of the 1st/2nd century AD, it resembles the lion in the British museum at London, famous for its inscriptions.

The riders on it are similar to the riders on elephants at Karle Cave and figures at the Sanchi gateway. It is a significant example of sculptural art of Haryana towards the beginning of Christian era. The coin moulds of the later Yaudheyas of 3rd/4th century AD have been discovered by the Archaeological Survey of India in large numbers. Of the same and subsequent dates are several clay seals. A Gupta period terracotta plaque and a head of a later date have also been discovered. The town continued to flourish till the 10th century AD, as coins of Samanta Deva, the Hindu king of Kabul, have been found here.

The town is said to have been rebuilt in the time of Prithviraj Chauhan. In 1828, General Mundy wrote about the 'ancient and consequently ruinous town' of Rohtak. The wide circuit of its dilapidated fortifications and the still elegant domes of many time-worn tanks tell melancholy tales of gone-by grandeurs.

At one time, the town had a wall all around with gates at regular intervals. Only three gates can now be seen but these are in a dilapidated condition. The town has a number of old mosques, some of which remind us of elegant Muslim structures. Dini Mosque or Adina Mosque is the oldest among these. At the north end of this mosque was a tehkhana (underground cell). Over its arch is an inscription of Ala-ud-Din Khilji, dating back to 1308. There is an old and mythical tank with ghats on three sides, known as Gaokaran tank. Its complex includes Shiva, Devi and Hanuman temples in addition to a park and a baradari.

Sirsa

Sirsa district has an area of 4,276 sq. km and its population is 9,03,000. The district headquarter is situated in Sirsa town. It is 255 km from Delhi and 280 km from Chandigarh. Other smaller towns are Dabwali, Ellenabad, Rori and Rania. The district lies between 29 14 and 30 0 north latitude and 74 29 and 75 18 east longitudes, forming the extreme west corner of Haryana. It is bounded by the districts of Faridkot and Bhatinda of Punjab in the north and north east, district Ganganagar of Rajasthan in the west and south and Hissar district in the east.

Sirsa district is divided into 3 subdivisions and 4 tehsils. There are a total of 323 villages in the district out of which 313 are connected with paved roads. About 79% of the population lives in the rural areas. Sirsa gets an annual rainfall of about 26 cm. The area under cultivation is 3,88,000 hectares out of which 3,06,000 is irrigated. The district excels in the production of cotton and citrus fruit.

Modern History: The Delhi territory along with districts of Bhattiana and Hissar was transferred to Punjab in 1858 and the district of Bhattiana was renamed as Sirsa. The Sirsa district which comprised three tehsils of Sirsa, Dabwali and Fazilka was abolished in 1884 and Sirsa tehsil (consisting of 199 Villages) and 126 villages of Dabwali tehsil formed one tehsil and the same was merged in the Hissar district and the rest of the portion was transferred to the Ferozepur district (Punjab). On September 1, 1975, Sirsa and Dabwali tehsils of Hissar district were constituted into a separate Sirsa district with headquarters at Sirsa. Ch Devi Lal's birthplace, the village of Chautala falls in this district.

Terrain of Sirsa may be classified into three types i.e. Haryana Plain, alluvial bed of Ghaggar or Nali and Sand dune tract. The Haryana Plain is a vast surface of flat to rolling terrain and extends south to the northern boundary of the bed of the Ghaggar. It covers over 65% area of the district. The elevation of the surface varies from 190 to 210 m. The palaeo channels set the occurrence of sand dunes in this terrain apart from those in the dune tract.

The plain is traversed by dune complexes and shifting sands. Alluvial bed of Ghaggar is a clayey surface of flat, plain bordered in the north and west by the Haryana Plain and in the south along the sound dune tract. Water logging is a serious problem in many parts due to impervious clay of great thickness. At places, swamps support a high density of tall grass. Sand dune tract is the southern most part of the district and is the northward extension of the sand dunes of Hissar and Ganga Nagar district of Rajasthan. Height of the Tibbas (sand dunes) vary from 13 to 17 m in some places. All tibbas are broad based transverse ridges, some more than 3 km long. Linear to complex ridges generally 2 to 5 m high are also present throughout the sandy stretch of the land.

Sonipat

The district headquarter is situated in Sonipat. Other smaller towns are Gohana, Ganaur, Murthal and Rai. The total area of Sonipat district is 2,260 sq. km and its population is 10,64,000. Sonipat is bordered by the states of Delhi and Uttar Pradesh as well as the districts of Rohtak, Jind and Panipat. The River Yamuna runs along the eastern boundary of the district. District Sonepat comprises of 3 subdivisions namely Ganaur, Sonepat and Gohana and seven blocks (Ganaur, Sonipat, Rai, Kharkhoda, Gohana, Kathura and Mundlana) has been carved out of Rohtak and made a full fledged district on 22 December 1972. Sonepat is the largest tehsil followed by Gohana.

Main water system in the district comprises of River Yamuna and the irrigation canals flowing out of it. There is no perennial river in the district. The underground water resources differ from area to area. The depth of the water table is the lowest in the Khader area along the Yamuna, where it is below 10 ft. It increases to 30 to 40 ft. in some of the western and south eastern part of the district. The ground water in some areas is saline and brackish. The ground water conditions indicate that the district faces the problem of occurrence of brackish water and water logging in eastern parts of the district.

Broadly speaking, the district is a continuous part of the Haryana-Punjab plain, but the area is not levelled in some parts. Over most of the district, the soil is fine loam of rich colour. However, some areas has sandy soil and others are comprised of Kallar. The plain has a gradual slope to the south and east. The district may be roughly divided into three regions:

(1) *The Khadar:* Along the River Yamuna is a narrow flood plain, 3 to 6 km wide, and is formed by the river along its course. The Khader plain is 20 to 30 ft. lower adjoining upland plain. It is comprised of fine clay loam left by the receding floods of the Yamuna. Presently, rice and sugar cane cultivation is undertaken by the farmers in the Khadar area. Recently, the farmers have started planting Banana, Pappaya and other fruits trees in this area.

(2) *The Upland Plain:* It consists of Sonepat tehsil lying to the west of the Khadar, and is the most extensive of the three regions: The Upland Plain is covered with old alluvium , which if properly irrigated, is highly productive. Extensive Farming of crops, oil seeds, horticultural plants, vegetables and flowers, is undertaken in this region. The ridges in Gohana tehsil represent the northern most extension of the Aravallis.

(3) *The Sandy Region:* A very smaller part of the district is covered with soil comprising of sand or sandy loam. Parts of this region has high PH value leading to kallor land.

Climate: Climate of Sonipat is dry with hot summer and a cold winter. The weather becomes milder during the monsoon (period July to September). The post-monsoon months October and November constitute a transition period, prior to the onset of winter.

Temperature: The winter starts in December when day and night temperatures fall rapidly. January is the coldest month when the mean daily minimum temperature is 6 to 7 Degree C. During cold waves, the minimum temperature may go down to the freezing point of water, and frosts can occur. During the summer months of May and June, the maximum temperature sometimes reaches 47 Degree Centigrade. Temperature drops considerably with the advancement of monsoon in June. However, the night temperature during this period continues to be high.

Humidity: Humidity is considerably low during the greater part of the year. The district experiences high humidity only during the monsoon period. The period of minimum humidity (less than 20%) is between April and May.

Rainfall: The annual rainfall varies considerably from year to year. However, the maximum rainfall is experienced during the monsoon season, which reaches it's peak in the month of July. In fact, the monsoon period accounts for 75% of the annual rainfall in the district. On an average there are 24 days in a year with rainfall of 2.5 mm (or more) per day in district Sonepat.

Wind: During the monsoon, the sky is heavily clouded, and winds are strong in this period. Winds are generally light during the post-monsoon and winter months.

Region Specific Weather Phenomena: Sonepat experiences a high incidence of thunder storms and dust storms, often accompanied by violent squalls (andhis) during the period April to June. Sometimes the thunder storm are being accompanied by heavy rain and occasionally by hail storms. In the winter months, fogs sometimes appear in the district.

Man Power: According the 1991 census the total population of the district is 10,45,158 Of this the urban population forms a small part and is 2,10,521. The district is primarily rural is in nature and the primary activity of the people is agricultural. The rural population of the district is 8,34,637. The male and female ratio in the rural areas is about 1:1 whereas the ratio in the urban areas is detrimental to the female population. The working population of district Sonepat according to 1991 census comprises of 11,50,49 cultivators, 58,296 agricultural laborers. The percentage of cultivators, to manufacturers is higher in sub-division Ganaur, whereas the actual number of agricultural laborers is higher in sub division Sonepat.

Soil Profile: District Sonepat, comprising of Sonepat, Gohana and Ganaur sub divisions, has 343 villages and covers an area of 2,13,080 hectares. The irrigated area (both with the help of canal irrigation as well as through tubewells) is 2,86,504 acres and the un-irrigated rainfed area is 43,979 acres. Sonepat is an important saltpetre producing area. The saltpeter appears as efflorescence on the surface during the summer season, specially in the village of Sonepat sub-division.

Water logging is a serious problem effecting the productivity of land. The water logged area, which the water table is between 0 to 5 ft, faces a serious problem. Where the water table is between 5 to 10 ft., the problem of water logging is imminent. There has been an alarming rise in the water table during the last two decades, Specially in the areas adjoining the canals. This has led to appearance of Thur on the surface of soil, followed by sem in several parts of the district, specially the areas adjoining the Yamuna and minor canals running through the district. The soil in Sonepat is rich and quite suitable for all types of agricultural crops as well as forest cover. The types of soil may be classified according to textures as : 1. Sandy (Raitali), 2. Sandy loam (Bhuri), 3. Loam (Rausli), 4. Clay loam (Karti) 5. Clay (Dakar). The main soil of the district is a good alluvial loam with sufficient moisture and is mostly rausli in texture.

Total No. of Villages	347
Inhabited	332
Uninhabited	15
Total Population	1045158
Male	5,67,901
Female	4,77,257

YAMUNANAGAR

District headquarter is situated in Yamunanagar. Other

smaller towns are Jagadhari, Chhachhrauli, Radaur and Sadhaura. Total area of the district is 1,756 sq. km and its population is 8,21,000.

Yamunanagar was formed as a new district of Haryana on 16 October, 1989. Earlier to that it was part of Ambala district. The river Yamuna forms its eastern boundary with the states of Uttar Pradesh and Uttaranchal. The district is also bordered by Himachal Pradesh and the districts of Karnal, Kurukshetra and Ambala. There are 655 villages and 10 towns in this district. Places to visit: Dadupur, Kalesar Forest, Hathni Kund and Tajewala barrage. Another not to be missed place is the Ch Devi Lal Herbal Park. Yamunanagar town has many large industries in plywood, paper, sugar, metal and utensils sector. Saraswati Sugar Mills is located here.

Kurukshetra

Haryana is home to important religious sites dating to Vedic times. With a battery of temples and pilgrim centres concentrated in the 48-*kosas* (92 miles) of land described in the epic *Mahabharata*, legend and mythology play an important role in the history of Kurukshetra, a place where the celestial song 'Bhagwad Gita' is believed to have been delivered by Krishna to Arjuna.

Kurukshetra town is situated 160 km north of Delhi on the national highway NH1. Other towns of the district are Pehowa, Ladwa, Ismailabad and Shahabad. The total area of Kurukshetra district is 1,682 sq. kms and its population is 6,41,000. Total area under cultivation is 1,68,000 hectares out of this, 1,47,000 is irrigated area. The Kurukshetra district lies between latitude 29o-52' to 30o- 12' and longitude 76o-26' to 77o-04' in the North Eastern part of Haryana State. The district has a total of 419 villages. Ghaggar, Markanda and Saraswati are the important rivers of the district.

Geography: The district is a plain which slopes generally from North East to South West. The plain is remarkable flat and within it, are the narrow low-lying flood plains, known as either Betre Khadar of Naili. A good network of canals is providing irrigational facilities. Underground water level is not relatively high. Tube well irrigation is also common in the district.

It is one of the prosperous district from agriculture point of view. Kurukshetra along with Karnal and Kaithal districts is known as the 'Rice Bowl of India' and famous for Basmati Rice. The soil is generally alluvial, loam and clay does not constitute average texture of the soil.

Climate of the district is very hot in summer (upto 47° C) and cold in winter (down to 1° C) with rains in July and August.

Kurukshetra is a place of great historical and religious importance, revered all over the country for its sacred association with the Vedas and the Vedic Culture. It was here that the battle of Mahabharata was fought and Lord Krishna preached his Philosophy of 'KARMA' as enshrined in the Holy Bhagvad Gita, to Arjuna at Jyotisar. In the very first verse of Bhagvad Gita, Kurukshetra is described as DHARAMKSHETRA i.e. 'Region of righteousness'. According to Hindu mythology, the name Kurukshetra applied to a circuit of about 48 KOS or about 128 Km which includes a large number of holy places, temples and tanks connected with the ancient Indian traditions and the Mahabharata War and Kurus, the ancestor of Kouravs and Pandavs. Kurukshetra is intimately related to the Aryan civilization and its growth along the Saraswati river.

Places to Visit: There are about 360 Tirthas of religious and historic importance. The foremoot among the Kurukshetra tirthas are Brahmsarovar or Kurukshetra Tank, Sannihit Tank, Sthanesvra Mahadev Mandir, Jyotisar, Baan-ganga, Bhisam Kund (Narkatari) Chandrakupa, Nabhi Kamal, Bhadarkali Mandir, Arnai Temple, Prachi Tirath Pehowa, Saraswati Tirath Pehowa, Prithduk Tirath Pehowa, Rantuk Yaksh Bir pipli, Karan Ka Tila,etc. A few archaeological sites which have yielded various objects of interest and a distinctive class of pottery known as the Painted Grey Ware (PGW) are Raja Karan Ka Tila, Asthipura, Bhor Saidan, Bhagpura and Daulatpur.

Kurukshetra is one of the very few places visited by all the Sikh Gurus and Gurdwaras have been erected to commemorate their visit, the most prominent among them being the Gurudwara Patshahi dedicated to the sixth Guru Hargobind. Hundreds of devotees visit this shrine every day whose design is simply marvellous.

The eighth Sikh guru Harkishan performed a miracle of making a deaf and dumb boy recite verses from the Bhagvad-Gita. The ninth Guru, Teg Bahadur, set camp near Sthaneshwar tirtha where a Gurudwara now stands. Gurudwara Rajghat, the biggest all the Kurukshetra Gurudwaras, is located near the main bank of the Kurukshetra tank. This was built in the memory of the Guru Gobind Singh who came here.

Tomb of Sufi saint Sheikh Chilhi Jalal is a fascinating monument, octagonal in shape, crowned with a dome of white marble and surrounded by a white marble courtyard. Also worth a visit are, Chini Masjid and Pathar Masjid.

Mahendergarh

Mahendergarh district was formed in 1948 by grouping different tracts of erstwhile princely states; Narnaul and Mahendergarh tehsils from Patiala State, Dadri (Charkhi Dadri) from Jind State and a part of Bawal nizamat from Nabha State. The headquarters of the district are at Narnaul.

Location: The district lies between north latitude 27^0 47 to 28^0 26 and east longitude 75^0 56' to 76^0 51'. It is bounded on the north by Bhiwani and Rohtak districts, on the east by Rewari district and Alwar district of Rajasthan, on the south by Alwar, Jaipur and Sikar districts of Rajasthan, and on the west by Sikar and Jhunjhunu districts of Rajasthan. It has 2 tehsils of Narnaul and Mahendergarh.

Total area	:	1,683 sq. km
Population	:	6,81,869
Narnaul	:	3,84,771
Mahendergarh	:	2,97,098
Total	:	6,81,869

Origin of the Name of the District: The Mahendergarh town was previously known as Kanaud which took its name from the Kanaudia group of Brahmans. It was founded by Malik Mahdud Khan, a servant of Babur. There is a fort at Mahendergarh which was built by Maratha Ruler, Tantia Tope during the 17th century. This fort was named as Mahendergarh in 1861 by Narinder Singh, the ruler of the erstwhile princely state of Patiala, in honour of his son, Mohinder Singh and consequently the town came to be known as Mahendergarh. The name of Narnaul Nizamat was changed to "Mahendergarh Nizamat".

Panchkula

Panchkula was formed as the 17th district of Haryana on 15th August, 1995. It comprises of two sub divisions and two Tehsils named Panchkula and Kalka. It has 264 villages out of which 12 villages are uninhabited and 10 villages wholly merged in towns or treated as census towns according to census 1991. There are four towns in the district named Kalka, Panchkula, Pinjore and HMT Pinjore. Area of the district is 816 sq. km and the total population is 3,19,398 out of which 1,73,557 are males and 1,45,841 females. The male literacy in the district is 61.8% whereas of the females is 46%.

Physical Aspects: Panchkula is surrounded by Himachal Pradesh in the north and north east by Ambala district in the east by Kurukshetra district in the south and Punjab and Union Territory of Chandigarh in the west.

Panchkula district has a sub tropical continental monsoon climate where we find seasonal rhythm, hot summer, cool winter, unreliable rainfall and great variation in temperature. In winter frost sometimes occurs during December and January. The district also receives occasional winter rains from the western disturbance. The rainfall is generally restricted to rolling plain in north and northeast a doom in Pinjore area and flood plain along the Ghaggar river. Morni hills constitute the highest point of the district as well as of Haryana.

The important rivers/streams of the district are Ghaggar, Sirsa nadi, Kaushalya etc. Generally the slope of the district is from north east to southwest in which direction most of the nadi/rivers rain fed torrents flow down and spread much gravels and pebbles in their beds. Only the Sirsa Nadi, in Kalka Tehsil, flows towards northwest through a u arrow halt of shivalik tract. The district is devoid of any perennial river. The soils in the district are mainly light loam (seoti) piedmont (Ghar and Kandi), Shivalik (pahar), silt clay (Naili and chhachhra Dakar) etc.

The under ground water in the district occurs under confirmed and semi-confirmed conditions which is generally fresh and suitable for domestic and irrigation purposes. The under ground water level is generally high in the southern parts and low in north and northeast which is hilly tract. The district lies in a region where earthquakes of moderate to high intensity had been felt in the fast. Being situated to Himalayan boundary fault zones it is prone to earthquakes.

The district has a favorable climate for the growth of rich and abundant vegetation due to reasonably good rainfall and elevation. Shisham (Dalbergia Sissoo), Kikar (Acacia nilotica) and Mango (Mangifera indica) are the important tree species grown in the plains. Safeda (eucalyptus hybrid) has been introduced since 1963 in forest areas as well as on private lands. The natural vegetation is mainly of forest growth in its degradation stages. Tropical dry and sub-tropical deciduous forests are found here.

Panipat

Panipat is situated on the banks of the river Yamuna, and here the three historical battles of Panipat were fought. This district is bordered by Karnal, Sonipat, Jind and Kaithal and the state of Uttar Pradesh.

The first battle of Panipat, fought in AD 1526 in which invader Babur defeated Ibrahim Lodhi, the Sultan of Delhi, on April 26. In the second battle of Panipat, on November 5, 1556, Akbar's guardian Bairam Khan defeated the Hindu ruler Hemu. Ahmad Shah Abdali, the Afghan ruler defeated the Marathas in the third battle of Panipat that took place on 13 January, 1761.

Today Panipat is an industrial town and is known for its handloom products. The district headquarter is situated in Panipat town. Other smaller towns are Samalkha, Israna and Naultha. The total area of Panipat district is 1,754 sq. km and its population is 8,33,000.

Ibrahim Lodhi's tomb: This king who was defeated by Babur in 1526 in the first battle of Panipat, lies buried here within a tomb. His grave is a simple affair; just a rectangular block on a high platform approached by a flight of steps made of lakhori bricks. The tomb was renovated by the British in 1866.

Kabuli Shah mosque was built by Babur after his victory over Ibrahim Lodhi.

He named the mosque after his wife Kabuli Begum. Six years later when Humayun defeated Salim Shah, he got a platform called Chabutara Fateh Mubarak made around the mosque. The mosque has chambers on two sides and an inscription in Persian runs along the parapet.

There are Jain temples in Holi mohalla and a shrine to the Muslim saint Abu Ali Kalandar. A fort rises up away from Panipat at its highest point, still guarding the city from invaders. There is a park named after the famous Urdu poet and critic Altaaf Hussain Haali, who was born in Panipat in 1837.

Hotels: Midtown hotel, phone 30769, a/c rooms and restaurant. Skylark motel, a/c rooms as well a dormitory and restaurant; Blue Jay and Kala Amb are also decent places for short stays. Also many smaller hotels and guest houses on GT road.

Rewari

Rewari became a district of Haryana on November 1, 1989. The district headquarter is situated in Rewari town. Rewari is 82 km from the national capital, New Delhi on the Delhi-Jaipur National Highway NH8. Rewari town is situated at an altitude of 241.95 m. Other smaller towns are Bawal, Dharuhera and Kosli. There are 412 villages in Rewari. The total area of Rewari district is 1,559 sq. km and its population is 6,23,000. This district borders the state of Rajasthan and the districts of Mahendergarh, Gurgaon and Rohtak.

Due to its proximity to Delhi and location on the Delhi-Jaipur national highway, Rewari has developed rapidly as an industrial hub. The district's economy has developed mainly around the Dharuhera Complex, Rewari Complex and the Bawal Growth Centre. The second manufacturing plant of Hero Honda Motors Limited, (the world's largest producer of two wheelers), is situated in the Dharuhera Industrial Area. Other major companies present in the district are Space Age India Ltd., Indo Nission Foods Ltd., Sony India Ltd., G.K. Invel Transmission Ltd., Pasupati Spining & Weaving Mills Ltd., Asahi India Safety Glass Ltd., Backton & Dickinson Ltd., and Svedala India Ltd.

Rewari also has a number of small scale industrial units engaged in manufacture of traditional items like Brass utensils, greystone bricks & tiles, and hand-made shoes (Tilla Jutis).

It is believed that during the Mahabharata period there was a king named Rewat who had a daughter whose name was Rewati. The king founded a city named 'Rewa wadi', after his daughter. Later Rewati got married to Balram, the elder brother of Lord Krishna. Much later the city Rewa wadi became known as Rewari. The red mosque (Lal Masjid) near the old courts is said to have been built during the regime of Mughal emperor Akbar in the year 1570.

Bhiwani

District Bhiwani was created on 22 July, 1972. The district headquarter is situated in Bhiwani town. Bhiwani has 442 villages, with main towns being Charkhi Dadri, Loharu, Bawani Khera and Tosham. The total area of Bhiwani district is 5,099 sq. kms and its population is 14,24,000.

Bhiwani district has many places worth visiting. Among these are the Star Building, Loharu Fort, Tosham Hill, Gauri Shankar temple, etc. An archaeological site at Naurangabad Mound, 10 kms from Bhiwani is now being excavated.

Member of Parliament: Sh Kuldip Bishnoi
Deputy Commissioner: Sh D D Gautam
Superintendent of Police: Sh A S Chawla
Chairperson Zila Parishad: Smt Seema Lamba

District Bhiwani is situated between 28.19 deg. & 29.05 deg. north latitude and 75.26 deg. and 76.28 deg. east Longitude. The Bhiwani district is surrounded by Hissar district on its north, some area of Jhunjunu & Churu district of Rajasthan on its west, Mahendergarh and Jhunjunu district on its south and district Rohtak on east. It is 124 kilometres from Delhi and 285 kilometres from Chandigarh.

In northern parts of the district are alluvial plains and in south is semi-desert with remnants of Aravali range hill. The soil is loam in the north and sandy in the southwest region. The ground-water is mainly saline with some of small pockets of fresh water in southwest.

The ground-water level of the district is decreasing fast. Lack of drainage system is the main cause of salinity of ground water. Temperature in Bhiwani varies from 1 Deg. C to 48 deg. C. Rainfall is scanty mainly in months of July and August.

Vegetation mainly thorny trees like Babul, Jandi, Kair, along with Neem, Sheesham, Peepal, etc. Crops like Bajra, Cotton in kharif and Wheat, Sarson in rabi. Minerals like building stone & Gypsum or flexible stones (Kaliyana village).

Bhiwani city finds mention in Ain-e-Akbari. It is claimed Bhiwani was founded by the Rajput name Neem after his wife named Bhani.

The Bhani word later changed to Bhiyani and subsequently to Bhiwani. Bhiwani has been a prominent centre of commerce since time of Mughals. Bhiwani is also known for its temples and is called as small Kashi of India because of numerous temples.

Another important city of the district is Dadri which was founded by the son of Prithvi Raj Chauhan. It is also a hub of commercial activity. For administrative purposes Bhiwani district is divided into six tehsils - Bhiwani, Bawani Khera, Dadri, Loharu, Tosham and Siwani.

Faridabad

The district headquarter is situated in Faridabad city. Other smaller towns are Ballabhgarh, Palwal and Hodal. The total area of Faridabad district is 2760 sq. kms and its population is 14,77,000. Faridabad city is the most populated and most industrialized in whole of Haryana.

The city is said to have been founded in 1607 AD. It is named after Sheikh Farid, Jahangir's treasurer, or Baba Farid, a Sufi saint.

One of the best place to visit is the Badhkal Lake, about 32 km from Delhi. This man-made lake is surrounded by Aravali Hills and there is a resort of Haryana Tourism to cater to the people visiting it.

The Surajkund Crafts Mela is held every year from Feb. 1 to Feb. 15. Surajkund is just 8 km from south Delhi on the Delhi-Agra national highway.

Fatehabad

The district Fatehabad, Haryana was formed on 15 July, 1997. The district headquarter is situated in Fatehabad town. Other smaller towns are Tohana, Ratia, Bhuna and Bhattu. The total area of Fatehabad district is 2,415 sq. km and its population is 6,15,000. There are facilities for stay at PWD rest house, HSEB rest house, market committee rest house and dharamsalas. The town is well provided with schools, college, hospital and other basic necessities.

The Fatehabad town was founded by the emperor Firoze Shah Tughluq and named after his son Fateh Khan in 1352 AD. The site on which the town was founded was a hunting ground. He dug a channel from the river Ghaggar in order to supply the town with water. He also built a fort which is now in ruins, the fortification walls can be seen on the east of the town. He also built three forts in the neighbouring villages in the name of his three sons. The old town was surrounded by a wall which has been dismantled to a great extent except near the fort.

Formerly, Fatehabad was an important trade centre for the export of surplus grain but with the construction of Rewari-Bhatinda railway line, which runs about 20 km to the west of the town, the trade shifted to Bhattu. But the town assumed greater importance after Independence when metalled roads provided important link and the earlier importance of the town was revived.

The two important monuments in Fatehabad are the Lat and the Humayun Mosque.

Lat or a stone pillar measuring about 5 m in height and 1.90 m in circumference at the base. It was erected in the centre of an Idgah. The lower portion of the pillar is a mono-block of light buff sandstone and is possibly the remaining part of the pillar that lies in the mosque at Hissar. It is more than likely that both these pillars once made a single monolithic pillar which was possibly erected by Ashoka at Agroha or Hansi. Firoz Shah Tughluq had a craze for taking away such columns and transplanting them among his favourite complexes. The Ashokan epigraph that was once engraved on the pillar was systematically chiselled off for writing the Tughluq inscription recording the genealogy of Firoz Shah in beautiful Tughra Arabic characters carved in high belief.

There are two inscriptions, one on a light coloured rectangular sandstone studded into the left of the screen-wall of Idgah, immediately behind or to the west of lat, praising the emperor Humayun and the other one is on a rectangular sand-stone placed on the outer wall of the mosque enclosure and contains a well-known invocation to Ali in Arabic. The mosque can still be seen in good conditions but lies in disuse.

Humayun Mosque is a small and a beautiful mosque. The legend assigns the association of the mosque to the Mughal Emperor Humayun who on his flight after his defeat at the hands of Sher Shah Suri happened to pass through Fatehabad on Friday and is said to have prayed at this mosque. The inscription praising Emperor Humayun was originally found here and later studded into the screen-wall of the Idgah. The mosque is said to have been repaired by one Nur Rehmat in the early eighties of the last century.

Two important archaeological sites have been found in this district. They are the Kunal Mound and the Banawali Mound. Both these sites seem to be a part of the Saraswati civilization of the Vedic times. The ancient mound of Banawali previously called Vanawali, lies 14 km, northwest of Fatehabad on the right bank of the Rangoi Nala at 29° 37" 5' north latitude and 75° 23" 6' east longitude. This proto-historic mound spread over an area of One sq. km, rise to a height of about 10 m due to successive settlements on the earlier rubble.

PINJORE GARDENS

Pinjore Gardens, also called Yadavindra Gardens are 20 km from Chandigarh, 15 km from Panchkula, on the Chandigarh Shimla road. Taxis and buses ply regularly between Pinjore, Kalka, Panchkula and Chandigarh. Pinjore lies on the foothills of the lower Shivalik ranges. The fascinating Mughal Gardens one of the most popular picnic spots. A mini zoo, plants nursery, a Japanese garden, historic palaces and picnic lawns await tourists. Especially at weekends, fountains are switched on and after dusk, lights pick up the beauty of the palaces by night.

Special programs are arranged at the Yadavindra Gardens for the Baisakhi (spring) festival in April and for the Mango Festival in June and July. A range of accommodation is available at Chandigarh, but a taste of royalty can be savored at Pinjore itself by a stay at the Yadavindra Gardens Budgerigar Motel, run by Haryana Tourism. A Bhima Devi Temple and an old baoli in the Pinjore town have legendary connection with Pandavs and Mahabharat.

The gardens have cool, shady walks and flagged pathways which run to the outer reaches of the creeper-covered walls. The end structure of the doorway has recently been made into a disc-like open-air theatre. The stiff outer wall of the garden is reminiscent of the fort walls, which has now all around dieter pavilions housing the zoo. Palm trees, shapely cypresses, Mango and dense groves of trees add a touch of mystery to the Yadavindra Gardens of Pinjore. A watercourse traipsing from level to level sparkles in the sunlight, its pools reflecting white shining pavilions and balconies etched high against a blue sky.

The graceful arched balconies and tinkling fountains, luxuriant green lawns and murmuring watercourse, limpid pools, shady walks and colourful flowerbeds, unusual descending terraces and monumental gateways—all were carefully planned to create a special effect.

Unlike other Mughal gardens, the seven terraces at Pinjore, instead of ascending, descend into the distance and achieve an almost magical effect. In the near distance, the purple-green Himalayas seem to rise up sheer over the battlements of the old garden walls and the white buildings of the little hill station of Kasauli in Himachal Pradesh, glow in the setting sun.

From the stately Sheesh Mahal built in the Rajasthani–Mughal style, the watercourse with its never-ending bubbling music cascades from terrace to terrace, flowing under the towering Rang Mahal, and then playing around the Jal Mahal. The structures date to the 17th century AD.

Nawab Fadai Khan, a great architect and foster brother of the Mughal emperor Aurangzeb is said to have designed the idyllic gardens. He planned the Gardens on the classical Charbagh pattern, giving the area a central water way. Both sides of this waterway were covered with patches of green bordered with flowers and shaded by trees.

He supervised the construction of the stylistic Sheesh Mahal (palace of glass), the Rang Mahal (painted palace), and the cube-like Jal Mahal (palace of water). After Fadai Khan's departure and the end of Mughal rule, these gardens he had so lovingly designed was overtaken by the wilderness. His Highness Maharaja Yadavindra Singh of Patiala (Punjab) is said to have restored Pinjore Garden to its former glory.

HATHNI KUND

A short drive from the town of Yamunanagar begins the Sal forest reserve of Kalesar. At Paonta Sahib the river Yamuna crosses over the last lap of the Himalayan foot hills. It flows into the plains of Haryana. And, the waters of the western Yamuna Canal are caught in the barrage at Tajewala. Each of these centres is within 5 km. The tourism centre of Haryana Tourism at Hathni Kund forms a link between these attractions.

Hathni Kund is a delightful location, Built on a raised plinth, the complex over looks the flowing waters of the Yamuna. In the far distance, stand the foothills of the Himalayas slowly blending into the skyline.

Hathni Kund is not the usual quiet retreat it seems at a glance. The summers bring groups of adventurous river rafters. Launching off on an expedition from Paonta Sahib, the rafts bob on till Hathni Kund. The rapids in this stretch are of medium intensity. Perfect for amateurs.

A number of expeditions have been run already. Adding a special appeal to rafting is the facility to camp out in the lawns of this complex. Rafting expedition, camping out at night and trekking in the Kalesar forest reserve are the major attractions.

Not only is the Kalesar forest a delight but so is the bird life. The tree pie, Drongo, Hornbills, Blue Peafowl, partridges will delight the ornithologist in you. Neelgai (Blue bull), Kakad or Barking deer, Monkeys, jackal and an occasional chital can also be spotted here. Kalesar covers about 5100 hectares and is the only Sal forest tract in Haryana. There are many flowering trees in the Kalesar forest, including Dhak, Kachnar and Amaltas.

The next halt can be made at an absolutely different location - the waterfront of Tajewala. The barrage at this location has fascinated many an angler, The waters have the Mahaseer for all those who care for this very restful experience. A permit is necessary. Obtain it from the Officer in charge. Special adventure club camps can be tailored to preference.

Facilities: Motel, restaurant rafting, camping, body surfing and wildlife tracts for adventure sport.

HARIKE WETLAND

Harike Lake and Wetland is situated in the districts of Kapurthala, Ferozepur and Amritsar in the state of Punjab. A barrage built in 1953 on the confluence of rivers Sutluj and Beas near Harike town resulted in the creation of Harike lake.

Over the course of time, this wetland system, the largest in north India, emerged as a fine waterfowl habitat. It was declared a bird sanctuary in 1982 and a Ramsar Site in 1990. In 1992 the sanctuary area was enlarged to 86 sq. km. Harike lake constitutes the main reservoir which is the deeper portion of the wetland adjoining the barrage, while the marshy islands and shores together with the extensive wetlands stretching beyond the reservoir area, comprise the rest of the wetland.

The lake is triangular in shape, with its apex in the west, a bund, called the Dhussi Bund forming one side, a canal the second and a major road the third. The Harike barrage connects Amritsar city with Ferozepur, Faridkot and Bhatinda by a national highway. Of the present sanctuary area, 73 sq. km constitutes a wetland enclosing shallow, marshy tracts that serve as perfect feeding and wading habitat for waterfowl. Tree covered earthen mounds have been constructed in the marsh area, to increase nesting sites for the birds.

Harike is a vital staging post and the winter home of a enormous concentration of migratory waterfowl that rivals only Keoladeo National Park near Bharatpur. Over 20, 000 ducks have been recorded here during the peak migratory season. A number of globally threatened species have also been recorded in Harike.

During the winter, about 200 species of birds visit the lake, including migratory as well as resident. From 1980-1985, the Bombay Natural History Society (BNHS) carried out research and a bird ringing program there. Harike was also the subject of a 1994 publication by WWF-India as part of their series on Ramsar Sites of India.

In addition to the common birds, other important species that can be seen here are Cotton Pygmy Goose, Tufted Duck, Yellow-crowned Woodpecker, Yellow-eyed Pigeon, Watercock, Pallas's Gull, Brown-headed Gull, Black-headed Gull, Yellow-legged Gull, Indian Skimmer, White-winged Tern, White-rumped Vulture, Hen Harrier, Eurasian Sparrowhawk, Eurasian Hobby, Horned Grebe, Black-necked Grebe, Great Crested Grebe, White-browed Fantail, Brown Shrike, Common Woodshrike, White-tailed Stonechat, White-crowned Penduline Tit, Rufous-vented Prinia, Striated Grassbird, Cetti's Bush Warbler and the Sulphur-bellied Warbler.

Some 7 species of turtle and 26 species of fish have been recorded in Harike. The mammals found at Harike include the Smooth Indian Otter, Jungle Cat, Jackal, Indian Wild Boar and the Common Mongoose. The rare and endangered Testudine Turtle and Smooth Indian Otter are listed in the IUCN Redlist of Threatened Animals. Harike attracts large populations of avifauna, in particular the diving ducks. It is a vital source of water for the people of Punjab. The main species of fish fauna present is Hilsa. The livelihood of nearby villagers depends to some extent upon the lake's fish resources.

Amongst phytoplankton, the *Bacillariophyceae* is represented by about 10 species. An extensive growth of *Typha elephantina* and *Phragmites karka* is observed along the margins of the lake, in surrounding low lying areas, as well as in the upstream Mand area. Of free floating plants, Azolla, the nitrogen fixing fern, occurs in patches of open water. The tall grasses *Saccharum spontaneum* and *S. bengalenses* are common along the higher ground in the wetland area and on slopes and margins of surrounding bunds and dykes. *Tamarix diocia* is the sole woody plant adapted to an aquatic habitat found in the area; rest of the trees are upland species.

The major threats to this important wetland include; large scale utilization of both surface and ground waters for irrigation, expansion of intensive agriculture resulting in encroachments on the wetland, drainage of agricultural chemicals into the waters, discharge of untreated waste from catchment towns into the rivers which feed the wetland, and deforestation of the lower Shivalik hills, causing soil erosion and silting.

The Indian Army in the year 2000, along with other agencies launched and completed a major project to clear water hyacinth, which was almost choking the lake.

BHINDAWAS SANCTUARY

Bhindawas Bird Sanctuary in district Jhajjar is around 15 km from Jhajjar town and is about 3 and a half hours drive from Delhi. The lake and the birds in it are the main attraction of this complex. The Sanctuary is spread over an area of 1074 acres which makes it considerably larger than the Sultanpur Bird Sanctuary.

The peripheral embankment is man made and basically constructed to store the escaped water of Jawaharlal Nehru canal through an escape channel at the time of power failure of Lift Canal System. The Bhindawas lake is being used by the migratory and resident birds of about 250 species. The best time to visit is December-January when you can view the maximum number of birds. The winter timings are 6:30 am - 5 pm and in summer from 6 am -6 pm. All in all, this is an excellent site for birders and bird watching.

The road to the lake is breathtaking, with acre upon acre of brilliant yellow mustard fields. There are many species of water birds near the canal even before reaching the sanctuary. A vehicle track goes all around the lake.

The government officials at the sanctuary are quite knowledgeable and keep a track of the various birds that visit the lake. There are two watchtowers on the edge of the lake, and the whole lake full of birds is visible from there. Even the areas surrounding the sanctuary have a large variety of birds. Since it is difficult to get close to these birds, photographing them is difficult unless one owns an expensive camera with powerful lenses.

The sanctuary is facing a big problem in the form of the weed 'water hyacinth', which has choked large sections of the lake. With the removal of water hyacinth, this sanctuary would attract many more birds. The state government has made some effort to clear this weed from the lake. Another problem is the drying up of this lake in periods of lean rainfall and/or shortage of water in the nearby canal. Haryana Tourism also needs to build a resort here to provide food and lodging to bird watchers who would like to spend the night here.

Blue Peafowl, Gray Francolin, Black Francolin, Graylag Goose, Ruddy Shelduck, Bar-headed Goose, Comb Duck, Gadwall, Eurasian Wigeon, Great Cormorant, Common Teal, Northern Pintail, Northern Shoveler, Red vented Bulbul, Common Pochard, Black-rumped Flameback, Common Hoopoe,

White-throated Kingfisher, Green Bee-eater, Black Drongo, Pied Cuckoo, Common Hawk Cuckoo, Rose-ringed Parakeet, Spotted Owlet, Blue Rock Pigeon, Great Egret, Purple Swamphen, Great Bittern, Eurasian Collared Dove, Mallard, Crested Lark, Jungle Babbler, Ashy Prinia etc are some of the more common birds found in this sanctuary.

In addition to the above birds, the antelope Neelgai (Blue Bull) and Jungle Cat can also be seen in this sanctuary.

RAKHIGARHI, KUNAL, AGROHA, BANAWALI

Rakhigarhi (Hissar District) 29.17N - 76.07E

Today, the 5000 year old history of our civilization is on the threshold of being rewritten. Recent excavations at Rakhi Garhi in Hissar district of Haryana may push the history of the civilization back by over a thousand years. This site could again bring to front, questions about the Vedic Civilization and its relationship to the Indus Valley civilization.

Archaeologists and historians are already excited about the findings from Rakhigarhi-a large site on the banks of, what is now believed to be, the dried bed of Saraswati river. Senior archaeologists consider this to be no ordinary Harappan site. They say the findings have already started showing new civilization contours.

Banawali (Fatehabad District) 29.36N - 75.25E

Banawali is a Pre Harappan and Harappan site. At Banawali, evidence of ploughed fields has been found. Large quantity of barley and evidence of growing of sesame and mustard have also been found. The use of wooden plough for ploughing the fields were prevalent. The mound in Banawali, 15 kms from Fatehabad, reveals a fortified town (BC 2500 – 1700).

Kunal (Fatehabad District) 29.38N - 75.43E

Kunal seems to be a Pre Harappan site. Two silver crowns presumably worn by the King and queen along with gold and silver jewellery has been found here in an earthen jar. This is the first time that a regal crown has been found in the subcontinent. This site brings to light that the Harappans went through three stages of development; from pit houses to regular rectangular and square dwellings above the surface.

Agroha (Hissar District)

The Agroha mound goes back to the 3rd century BC and is where Harappan coins were discovered apart from stone sculptures, terracotta seals, iron and copper implements, shells and a host of other things.

Mittathal (Bhiwani District) 28.52N - 76.11E

At this site, three phases of Harappan culture have been found.

Naurangabad (Bhiwani District)

Remains of a town about 2500 year old have been found here.

STAR MONUMENT

Star monument is one of the most breathtaking buildings in Haryana. This building houses the samadhi of Sh Tara Chand fondly called 'Maharaj ji' by his followers. The building is situated in the Radhaswami Satsang Bhawan complex, Dinaud, about 12 km from Bhiwani, Haryana.

The monument is a hexagonal pyramid, with its sides being in the shape of a star, as Maharaj ji's first name 'Tara' means a star. The height from the base platform is 88 feet, while the platform itself is raised 6 feet. Each of the six sides' measure about 60 feet at the base. Out of the six, three alternative sides are covered in white marble while the other three in Italian glass. The samadhi of Maharaj ji is inside the building in the centre of the floor. A unique thing about the design of this building is that it doesn't have pillars or columns to support it.

There is a small beautifully landscaped garden around the monument. The garden houses the small hut in which Maharaj ji used to meditate. The building is not yet complete as some minor works remains to be done and it is expected to be fully completed by September, 2001. The whole cost of constructing this monument was borne by the followers of Maharaj ji living in India and abroad.

The Haryana government needs to develop the immediate area around the building and repair roads so that this spot can become one of the major tourist attractions of Haryana.

8

Population and Religion

POPULATION OF HARYANA

Haryana is one of the 29 states in the nation, situated in North India. It was removed of the past territory of East Punjab on 1 November 1966 on an etymological premise. The state is flanked by Punjab and Himachal Pradeshtoward the north and by Rajasthan toward the west. The Yamuna stream portrays its eastern outskirt with Uttar Pradesh.

Haryana incorporates the country's capital Delhi on three sides, confining the northern, western and in addition southern fringes of Delhi. In this manner, a tremendous territory of south Haryana is consolidated into the National Capital Region for reasons making arrangements for development. The state is additionally known for its farmland sees.

As indicated by the 2011 enumeration, Hindus (87.45%) constitute most of the state's population with Sikhs (4.91%), Muslims (7.03%).

Talking about population, in order to check out the population of Haryana in 2018, we need to have a look at the population of the past 5 years. They are as per the following:

1. 2013 – 26.1 Million
2. 2014 – 26.5 Million
3. 2015 – 26.9 Million

4. 2016 – 27.6 Million
5. 2017 – 27.96 Million

Predicting the 2018 population of Haryana is not easy but we can get the idea after analysing the population from the year 2013 – 17. As we have seen that every year the population increases by approximate 0.372 Million people. Hence, the population of Haryana in 2018 is forecast to be 27.96 Million + 0.372 Million = 28.332 Million. So, the population of Haryana in the year 2018 as per estimated data is 28.332 Million.

Haryana Population 2018 –28.332 Million. (estimated).

Demography Of Haryana

Jaats shape the biggest position in the state with about 25% population. Out of 80 castes, 63 castes have been informed as a Scheduled Caste or Backward Class in the state. In terms of reservation limit, it remains at 47%. Muslims are essentially found in the Mewat and Yamuna Nagar regions, while Sikhs live generally in the region abutting Punjab, and Sirsa. Its sex proportion crossed the characteristic mark of 903 in December 2015. As of religion, Hinduism rules at 87.45%, trailed by Islam and Sikhism.

Population Density And Growth Of Haryana

The population density is 573 persons per square kilometre. Compared to 28.43% in the 1991-2001 periods, Haryana has recorded a population development of 19.90% in the midst of 2001-2011 when stood out from 28.43% in the prior decade of 1991-2001. The share of its population in the country's total population has extended from 2.06 to 2.09%.

While the total population has risen from 21,144,564 in 2001 to 25,353,081 in 2011, the number of males has gone up from 11,363,953 to 13,505,130 in the year 2011. Similarly, the number of females shot up from 9,780,611 to 11,847,951 in 2011.

Facts About Haryana:

1. There are various amounts of Steel, Plywood and Textile Industries in this state. It has India's greatest maker of bicycle and cars.
2. The temperature of the state sways between 15 degree Celsius to 5 Celsius amid winter and 15 degree Celsius to 45 degree Celsius amid the mid year.
3. It is all around associated by means of railroads and road framework. Haryana furthermore is all around associated with air routes as well.
4. Haryana is seen as one of the wealthier states of the nation. A significant part of the cultivating, vehicles and distinctive businesses are arranged in Haryana.
5. The state of Haryana is bordered by Himachal Pradesh, Punjab, Rajasthan, Uttarakhand and Uttar Pradesh moreover with River Yamuna. The state fringes the Country's capital Delhi on its three sides.

DEMOGRAPHICS AND RELIGION

Demographics

The population of Haryana, according to the 2001 census, is 21, 144, 000, with 11, 364, 000 males and 9, 781, 000 females.

The population density is 477 people/sq. km. Haryana, along with neighbouring Punjab, has a skewed sex ratio, with many more men than women. Selective abortion of female foetoses is known to occur. These problems have lead to a shortage of brides and are contributing to the purchase of brides from Orissa, Jharkhand, and Bihar.

Hindus make up about 88% of the population, Sikhs 6%, Muslims 6%, Jains 0.3% and Christians 0.1%. Muslims are mainly in the Mahendergarh district, while Sikh's are mostly in the districts adjoining Punjab.

The northern districts have significant Punjabi population, while the southern and central districts have Jaat majority.

Religion in Haryana (2011)

Hinduism (87.46%)

Islam (7.03%)

Sikhism (4.91%)

Jainism (0.21%)

Christianity (0.20%)

Buddhism (0.03%)

Others (0.18%)

According to the 2011 census, of total 25,350,000 population of Haryana, Hindus (87.46%) constitute the majority of the state's population with Muslims (7.03%) (mainly Meos) and Sikhs (4.91%) being the largest minorities.

Muslims are mainly found in the Mewat and Nuh districts. Haryana has the second largest Sikh population in India after Punjab, and they mostly live in the districts adjoining Punjab, such as Hisar, Sirsa, Jind, Fatehabad, Kaithal, Kurukshetra, Ambala, Narnaul and Panchkula karnal.

LAND

Area	: 44, 212 Sq. Km
Capital	: Chandigarh
Districts	: 19
Language	: Hindi
Population	: 21, 082, 989
Males	: 11,327,658

The state of Haryana is bounded by Uttar Pradesh in the east, Punjab in the west, Himachal Pradesh in the north and Rajasthan in the south. The Union Territory of Delhi juts into Haryana and is encompassed by it on three sides. The south west of the Haryana is dry sandy and barren. The natural boundaries are: the Shivalik hills in the north, River Yamuna in the east and river Ghaggar in the west.

The south western boundary is provided by the range of Aravali hills, which run through southern Delhi and the Gurgaon district up to Alwar. There are some high ridges running from the northwest to southeast with numerous spurs branching out in all directions. These hills are known as the Morni and Tipra ranges. They belong to the outer ranges of the Himalayas.

Rivers: Haryana has no perennial rivers. The important rivers are Yamuna, the Saraswati and the Ghaggar. Several small streams flows through the state they are the Markanda, the Sahibi and Indori. Yamuna is the most important river in the state. It has its source in the hills at Kalesar and is the source of irrigation for large tracts in the districts of Ambala, Kurukshetra, Karnal, Hissar and Rohtak through the western Yamuna canals.

The river Saraswati begins in the large depression at Kalawar in the north of the Mustafabad Pargana of Jagadhri. The Ghaggar rises in the outer Himalayan ranges between the Yamuna and the Sutlej.

The climate of Haryana over most of the year is of a pronounced continental character. It is very hot in summer and markedly cold in winter. The rainfall in the region is low and erratic except in parts of the Karmal and Ambala districts.

The rainfall is unevenly distributed during the year except for two well marked seasons. One is the monsoon period lasting from the middle of June to the end of September on which autumn crop and spring sowing depend and the other is the winter rains which occur from December to February, benefiting rabi crop. Rainfall is meager, particularly in the districts of Mahendergarh and Hissar.

SOIL

Soil is formed almost entirely of alluvium, the state is situated towards the depressions of the rivers Ganges and Indus. It is a broad level plain standing nearly on the watershed between the basins of the two rivers. It is a vast ground of moist land. In the whole of the region except the flood plains of the Yamuna and the Ghaggar, the alluvium is of the old type containing sand, clay, silt and hard calcareous concentrations about the size of nuts known as 'Kankars'.

In the Khaddar the deposits of the alluvium are the recent type. They consist of coarse sand and some silt regularly deposited by the rivers and small mountain streams of the Indo-Gangetic watershed.

DISTRICTS OF HARYANA

S.No	District	Area in Sq Km	Population	Headquarter
1.	Ambala	1,574	10,13,660	Ambala
2.	Bhiwani	4,778	14,24,554	Bhiwani
3.	Faridabad	2,151	21,93,276	Faridabad
4.	Fatehabad	2,520	8,06,158	Fatehabad
5.	Gurgaon	2,766	16,57,669	Gurgaon
6.	Hissar	3,983	15,36,417	Hissar
7.	Jhajjar	1,834	8,87, 392	Jhajjar
8.	Jind	2,702	11,89,725	Jind
9.	Kaithal	2,317	9,45, 631	Kaithal
10.	Karnal	2,538	12,74,843	Karnal
11.	Kurukshetra	1,530	8,28,120	Kuruksehtra
12.	Mahendergarh	1,859	8,12,022	Narnaul
13.	Panchkula	898	4,69,210	Panchkula
14.	Panipat	1,268	9,67,338	Panipat
15.	Rewari	1,582	7,64,727	Rewari
16.	Rohtak	1,745	9,40,036	Rohtak
17.	Sirsa	4,277	11,11,012	Sirsa
18.	Sonepat	2,122	12,78,830	Sonepat
19.	Yamuna Nagar	1,768	9,82,369	Yamuna Nagar

In the southwestern part, a great deal of wind-blown sand has been piled up in the form of sand dunes. These dunes are some times many metres high and extend many kilometres in length. The alluvium is covered by sand, making the region as arid and unproductive as a desert.

The only part useful for cultivation in this region are Tals, where due to some reason or the other sand does not collect.

The district headquarter is situated in Ambala City. Other towns are Ambala Cantt., Barara, Naggal, Mulana, Saha and Shahzadpur. The total area of Ambala district is 1569 sq. km and its population is 11, 06, 000. It is famous for its big army cantonment, air force base and a very busy railway junction. There are a number of stories regarding the name 'Ambala'.

According to one, this town was founded in the 14th century by one Amba Rajput. According to another the town is named after the Goddess Bhawani Amba. Yet another stories claims that the town was originally called Amb Wala (place of Mangoes), and over time this got corrupted into the present name of Ambala.

In 1841, after an outbreak of malaria, the British abandoned the cantonment at Karnal. In its place a large cantonment was founded in Ambala in 1843. Ambala district is famous for its industries, especially that of scientific instruments, metal casting, kitchen mixer grinders and submersible motor pumps. There are many shrines in and around Ambala City.

There is a temple, Bhawani Amba, named after the goddess Bhawani. The Badshahi Bag Gurudwara, Sis Ganj Gurudwara, Manji Sahib Gurudwara, Sangat Sahib Gurudwara are the historical Gurudwaras here. These are associated with Guru Gobind Singh, Guru Tegh Bahadur and Guru Hargobind respectively.

PEOPLE

Haryana has been the hub of social, cultural and religious activity in India, even before the time of Vedic Civilization. Given its unique geography, the state of Haryana was witness to the invasions of the Muslim rulers, battles of the Marathas and the Sikhs. Hindu saints, Buddhist monks and Sikh gurus have traversed Haryana, spreading their messages of universal love and brotherhood. The population of Haryana, according to the 2001 census, is 2, 10, 83, 000, with 1, 13, 28, 000 males and 97, 55, 000 females. The population density is 477 people/sq. km.

People of Haryana are simple, straightforward, enterprising and hard-working. Since ancient times, they have survived many upheavals upholding the traditional glory and greatness of the land to this day. They have preserved their ancient Vedic traditions. They celebrate festivals with great enthusiasm and traditional fervour. The region has its festivals, popular folklores, folksongs and musical instruments. The women are devoted and diligent and assist their menfolk on the farms. The people have simple food habits. They are known for their love for cattle and the abundance of milk and curd in their diet.

Religion has always provided the main basis for the structure of the Haryana society. In ancient times, Aryan people followed the Vedic religion. Later on Buddhism, Jainism, Islam and Sikhism influenced the people. Swami Dayanand's teachings greatly impressed the people and the Arya Samaj has a large following among Hindus of Haryana. In present day Haryana, Hindus are about 90% of the population, Sikhs 6.2%, Muslims 4.05% and Christians 0.10%. Hindus are divided into a number of castes like Jats, Brahmins, Ahirs, Gujars, Aggarwals, Arora Khatris, Sainis, Rajputs and Rors. Among them all, the Jats occupy a preeminent position in Haryana, being the largest group in the state. The artisan castes such as Telis (oil traders), Sunars (goldsmith), Lohars (blacksmiths), dhobis (launderers) and Nais (barbers) are found throughout the state, especially in villages.

The Jats are spread throughout Haryana. The origin of Jats is shrouded in mystery. Harijans constitute about one fifth of the population. As a result of various facilities and privileges provided by the Government, the Harijans are now taking a active part in all the activities. The Muslims in the state are mostly Meos and are concentrated in the Mewat region. Although Islam does not preach casteism, there are three categories of Muslims in Haryana. The Asharf or Sharaf (noble) form the higher caste, the Ajlaf (base or mean) is the middle with Arzal (lowest of all) coming at the end. There are Muslim Rajputs as well as converted Muslims. The Sikhs generally live in Ambala, Kurukshetra and Karnal districts. Sikhs too have their own castes like Jat Sikhs, Aroras etc.

More than 70% of the population is depended on agriculture for their livelihood. The people speak several similar sounding dialects of Hindi. The most important dialect being 'Bangaru'. The people of Haryana are generally speaking taller, stronger and healthier than the average Indian due to hard work and the inclusion of lots of dairy products in their diet. The main languages spoken by the people are Haryanavi, Hindi, Panjabi, Urdu and English. Sanskrit is now taught in schools till the 8th class.

Bravery Awards: Param Vir Chakra & Maha Vir Chakra winners from Haryana, India

Param Vir Chakra

1. Colonel Hoshiar Singh PVC (Grenadiers) IC-14608

Maha Vir Chakra

01. Captain Devinder Singh Ahlawat MVC IC-19161
02. Brigadier V. P. Airy MVC IC-7750
03. Maj Gen Madan Mohan Singh Bakshi MVC IC-1697
04. Lt Colonel I. J. S. Butalia MVC IC-159
05. Major M. S. Chaudhary MVC IC-8164
06. Major Vijay Rattan Chaudhary MVC IC-11004
07. Lt. General R. S. Dyal MVC IC-4004
08. Lt. Colonel Dharam Singh MVC IC-2447
09. Lance Naik Hari Singh MVC 4476
10. Havildar (Hony. Caption) Fateh Singh MVC 12742
11. Wing Commander Jag Mohan Nath MVC 3946 F(P)
12. Lt. General Khem Karan Singh MVC IC-2041
13. Maj Gen Swarup Singh Kalaan MVC IC-219
14. Sepoy Man Singh MVC 4128692
15. Brigadier Rai Singh Yadav MVC IC-5086
16. Naik Shishpal Singh MVC 3131692
17. Leading Seaman Chaman Singh Yadav MVC 87000
18. Commodore B. B. Yadav MVC 00101 B

19. Lt. Col Sardul Singh Randhawa MVC IC-2658
20. Lt. Colonel H. S. Virk MVC IC-665

Jats

Jats occupy a preeminent position in Haryana, western Uttar Pradesh, Punjab, Delhi and eastern Rajasthan, being the largest group in northwestern India. They are divided into 12 clans and about 300 gotras. Though the origin of Jats is shrouded in mystery, they are believed to be an Indo-Aryan tribe, connected to the Vedic civilization (4500 BC - 2500 BC) that existed along the Saraswati River.

Even today, the highest density of Jat population is along the dried bed of Saraswati, starting from Haryana, going on to Punjab and ending up in Rajasthan.

They play a predominant role in this region. Agriculture, soldiering and cattle rearing have been the main occupation of the Jats, but now they are branching out in other fields like military and police. They are also well represented in government civil services.

Though the common definition refers to only the Hindu Jats, a significant number of Jats are Sikhs and Muslims. The Jats are not a homogeneous ethnic group living in a particular area and speaking a single language. Rather, they are a people who live scattered around the world among several ethnic groups, yet retain their own identity. This distinction is often based on occupation and heritage.

The Jats are primarily located in north India and southern Pakistan, although there are said to be some communities in Germany, Denmark, Sweden, Russia, Iran and Ukraine. However, their origin, history, and current dispersion are spread much wider. They are said to be of Indo-Aryan (or often, Indo-Scythian) descent. History proves that they reached Egypt with the Muslim conquerors, lived in Afghanistan before the Muslims, and invaded China with the Mongol army. They also proved to be a threat to Tamar Lane in Persia and Uzbekistan.

There is also a theory suggesting that they may be the predecessors of Gypsies. Whatever their origin, in the eighteenth century, the Jats became a force that could not be ignored. Jats are a brave, hardworking and independent minded people. Primarily agriculturists, the Jats led a fairly autonomous political life. Even during the Mughal period, the rule of the state was limited. With the exception of Bharatpur, no Jat kingdoms were founded.

As per the Varna (Caste) system, the Jats are Kshatriyas or the warrior class. As they were outside the rigorous brahmanical social order, this position was not emphasized till the growth of the Arya Samaj among the Jats. Overall, the Jats have a very good self image and they are a proud people. 'Men may come and men may go, but I go on forever, ' is a well known Jat proverb. They are brave, hardworking people who possess both the desire and ability to rule. It has been said that no Jat wants to be ruled. Rather, he desires to have power over a group, if not over an area.

The first opposition to Aurangzeb's autocratic rule came from the Jats of Mathura. In 1669, the sturdy and hard working peasantry of Jats under the leadership of Gokla, zamindar of Tilpat, rose against and killed the Imperial Faujdar Abdun-Nabi. It took more than one year for the powerful Mogul forces to subdue the Jats. Gokul was killed and his family forcibly converted to Islam.

But this did not deter the Jats and they once again rose in rebellion in 1685 under the leadership of Raja Ram. Akbar's tomb in Sikandra was plundered by them in 1688. Finally the Jats were defeated and Raja Ram slain in 1691. But the brave Jats again got organized under the leadership of Churaman and revolted. They continued a strong armed resistance against the Mughals after Aurangzeb's death.

Towards the end of Aurangzeb's reign, bands of Jats under individual leaders like Rajaram, Bhajja and Churaman carried out depredations around Delhi and Agra. They slowly increased their power. But whatever they had achieved was lost when Sawai Jai Singh II captured Churaman's stronghold of Thun in 1721.

Till this time Jats were never united and they followed their individual village headsmen. But all this was changed by Badan Singh, the son of Churaman's brother, Bhao Singh. Even in the face of great difficulties, Badan Singh established his authority over almost of Agra and Mathura by wisdom, versatility and marriage alliances with powerful Jat families. Badan Singh died on 7th June, 1756. His adopted son and successor was Suraj Mal.

Suraj Mal, has been variously described as 'Plato of Jat tribes' and 'Jat Ulysses' because of his sagacity, steady intellect and clear vision. Suraj Mal extended his kingdom to Agra, Mathura, Dholpur, Mainpuri, Hathras, Aligarh, Etawah, Meerut, Rohtak, Farrukhnagar, Mewat, Rewari and Gurgaon.

He was described as the greatest warrior and the ablest statesman that the Jats have produced. Suraj Mal died on 25th December, 1763. Such was the might of the Jats that Bharatpur came to be known as the impregnable city.

The beautiful palace and gardens at Deeg and the Bharatpur fort, both built by Suraj Mal , symbolized the coming of age of the Jat state.

Soon, nobody dared question the Jats' prowess in battle. A British general, Lord Lake, thought otherwise and paid dearly with his life for his decision to besiege the Lohagarh fort. At Deeg, the maharaja's men successfully took on the might of a combined Mughal and Martha army of 80, 000. Growing from strength to strength, the Jats even dared to attack the Red Fort in Delhi, the ultimate icon of power.

Known for their military prowess, many Jats were recruited into the British-India Army during World War I. Before that, they served as fighters in the Persian army. A large number of Jats serve is in the Indian Armed Forces and form one of the largest ethnic groups in the army. The late Colonel Hoshiar

Singh PVC, winner of the highest military award, the Param Vir Chakra came from a Jat family of Haryana.

The Green Revolution brought considerable prosperity to the Jats in the late 60s and 70s. The Jat regions in India are among the most prosperous on a per-capita basis. Today, many Jats are well read and some occupy high positions in academic and technical arenas. Conservative by nature, the Jats rarely marry people from other ethnic groups. Great pride is placed in their ancestry. In fact, all the Jats in a particular village consider themselves to be the descendants of the man whom they believe founded it. Most Jats in India are Hindus, the rest being Sikhs or Muslims. The Jats living in Pakistan are primarily Muslim.

The Hindu Jats' religious beliefs are usually non-orthodox. A large number came under the influence of Swami Dayanand and the Arya Samaj in the early part of the 20th century. The Arya Samaji influence played a significant role in shaping the socio-religious identity. Until recent times, the Sikh Jats seemed to be the least meticulous in their observance of Sikh traditions, leaning more towards Hinduism. The Muslim Jats are Sunnis of the Hanafi School, but are known to have a strong tradition of worshipping many local saints.

Sir Chhotu Ram and Chaudhary Devi Lal (former Deputy Prime Minister of India), are the two most famous Jat leaders from Haryana. Seth Chhajju Ram was one of the most successful business man and philanthropist. Colonel Hoshiar Singh PVC won India's highest military medal, the Param Vir Chakra. Lt. Gen Khem Karan Singh MVC was another great Jat soldier from Haryana and won the Maha Vir Chakra. Mallika Sehrawat, a very popular movie actress, comes from a well known Jat family of Haryana.

Ahirs

Ahirs, Yadavs or Yadavas are to be met with throughout the country especially in Haryana. They include the Abhiras or Ahirs of northern India, Raos of Haryana, Gwallas of Uttar Pradesh, Mandals of Bihar, Pradhans of Orissa, Yadavs of Rajasthan, Ghoshals of Bengal, Gopas and Reddis of Andhra Pradesh and Wadeyars of Karnataka. High-caste Hindus often call them Sudras but the Yadavas call themselves Somavanshi Kshatriyas. The Yadava contribution to the composite culture of India is immense: the nomadic art forms, the Abhira language (Apabhramsa), the Raslila and certain ragas life Ahir-Bhairav, Abhirika, Gopixa, Kannadaguala and perhaps most of all, the Krishna cult.

Although the Ahirs and Yadavas form one group, the former (the Ahiras or Abhiras) are an important community of Haryana, but numerically they constitute less than 10 % of the total population.

Most of them live in the region around Rewari and Narnaul which is therefore known as Ahirwal or the abode of Ahirs. Their origin is controversial. Some historians hold that they were a powerful race of nomad cowherds from eastern or central Asia who entered India from the Punjab in large hordes about the same time as the Sakas and the Yuehchis in 1st or 2nd century BC and gradually spread over large parts of northern, eastern and central India.

Other views are that they came from Syria or Asia Minor about the beginning of the Christian era; were Dravidians; sprang from the Aayars of Tamil Nadu; lived in India long before the Aryan invasion; were descendants of the Yadavas of the Lunar family of Pururavas Aila; and that their original habitat was the region between the Sutluj and the Yamuna from where they migrated beyond Mathura in the east and beyond Gujarat and Maharashtra in the South.

The Ahirs of Mathura and Bajra regions were known to be peace loving cowherds whereas the Abhirs of Haryana and Mahendergarh, who later on became to be called as Ahirs, were powerful and accomplished warriors. The generations from the kidnapped women or widows were known as Yaduvanshis.

However, the ones with Abhir fathers became to be known as Yadavs. Out of these Yadavs, many have been categorized into backward classes whereas the rest of them are flourishing farmers in Haryana, Uttar Pradesh, Bihar and Rajasthan states.

The name of Haryana may have been derived from its ancient inhabitants: Abhirayana == Ahirayana == Hirayana == Haryana. The name 'Abhira' may stem from a-bhira—a, not; bhira, fear— fearless The Ahir hold over Haryana must have remained intact for centuries after the battle of the Mahabharata.

At the beginning of the Christian era the invading Scythians and Kushans forced most of them out of their land to lower Rajasthan in the Arbuda (Aravali region). In Marubhumi (Marwar), Saurashtra and Maharashtra they served the local rulers and established their own Raj. Ishwar Sena, a great Ahir general, became master of western Deccan in place of the famous Satavahanas.

He took the title of Rajan and an era was named after him. His descendants continued to rule for nine generations. For centuries the Ahirs were eclipsed as a political power in Haryana until the time of the Pratihera dynasty. In time they became independent rulers of southwestern Haryana.

Rao Tula Ram was the most well known of the Ahir leaders. He fought against the British in the 1857 revolt. Many brave Ahir soldiers from Haryana have made their mark in the various wars fought by the Indian Army and won medals. Among them are Brigadier R. S. Yadav MVC, Commodore B. B. Yadav MVC and Leading Seaman C. S. Yadav MVC.

Gurjars or Gujjars

The Gujars belong to the northwestern parts of India like Gujarat, Rajasthan, Himachal Pradesh, Jammu & Kashmir, Uttar Pradesh, Uttaranchal, Haryana, and Punjab. They are mostly Muslims, the rest being either Hindus or Sikhs. Gujarat is said to be named after them as they settled there in the 6th century AD. There are 15 lac Gurjar Muslims in Jammu & Kashmir. Gurjars saved Kashmir during first invasion of Pakistan when Pakistan annexed the area, called Pakistan Occupied Kashmir (POK). Three Muslim Gurjars (nomads) including one woman were awarded Padma Shree by the President of India for this act of patriotism.

The Muslim Gujars are divided into two sections, the Bhatariye and the Bhanariye who do not usually intermarry. The Hindu Gujars are usually divided into three groups: Gujar, Dodhi Gujar and Bakarwal. Originally Gujars are thought to be an Aryan tribe that entered India in parts of Gujarat and Rajasthan from North West. Having been cattle breeders and milkmen, they were usually associated with herdsmen and shepherds. Traditionally they were a pastoral people with no fixed abode. A large number of Gujars have now settled down and taken to farming and combine agricultural work with animal husbandry.

Gujars in Uttar Pradesh and Uttaranchal are found both in Himalayan foothills and on the plains in the Rohilkhand area. Groups camp in the forests of Dehradun and Saharanpur districts in winter from November to March. They migrate with herds of buffalo and cattle to the Himalayan summer pastures in Shimla district (Himachal Pradesh) or Tehri Garwhal & Uttarkashi, (Uttaranchal) for the months of April to October.

In mid-April they gather to await permission to travel, which is given by the state government. They are able to graze their herds on the stubble of the villagers' fields, but conflict often arises with villagers on the route as from whom they have to obtain wheat and other supplies by exchange of milk.

They take ten to twenty days on each journey on fixed routes away from roads and villages. Each family has on average from 22 to 32 buffaloes. Summer pastures are at 2, 500 m (8, 000 ft) and higher. On the return many take the cattle of villagers to care for them on the plains and return them in the spring.

In Haryana they are settled in Faridabad and Panchkula districts and the Samalkha segment of Panipat district. They are simple, thrifty and industrious. The Gujars are cultivators only in the plains but in the hills they are more given to keeping cattle than following the plough.

Brahmins

The Brahmins of Haryana are divided into four main groups: Gaurs, Saraswats, Khandelwals and Dhima. The Gaurs claim that they come originally from Bengal. But is believed they came as Purohitas of the various immigrant farming tribes. The Saraswats are original settlers of this region, taking their name from the Saraswati River.

The Khandelwals and Dhima came into this region later, most probably from neighbouring Rajasthan. The Brahmins themselves had a ranking system between them with the Gaurs being on the top followed by the Saraswats, the Khandelwals and the Dhima. The Gaurs used to consider themselves to be superior to the other Brahmins and neither ate, drank nor intermarried with them.

The Brahmins have lived in every village and town of Haryana. In earlier times most of them were working as *Purohitas* (priests), though some of them were also engaged in agriculture. The Brahmins were held in high esteem by the people due to their high socio-religious status. In the pre-partition pre-independence days they formed about 8% of the total population of the region.

Sainis

Sainis claim to be an ancient Vedic Kshatriya tribe. They are now a farming caste and generally avoid priestly duties, business etc. They claim descent from Rajan Saini (called 'Sini' in texts) and his grandson Satyaki of the Mahabharata fame.

They founded 'Saini Vamsh' of the Sura-Sena which is one of the eleven Vamshas of Krishna and one of the tribes of the

Yadavas. The descendants of Avamitra, the youngest son of Vrsihni are called Sainyas through his son Saini. Satyaki and Yuyudhana are born from this family. Sainis are said to have been cursed to be kingless and used the title of Rajan but rarely Raja. Yadu too had a curse for rebelling against his father Yayati.

Sainis are spread along the Shivalik foothills from Gurdaspur on Ravi (Punjab), through Haryana to Haridwar (Uttaranchal). Reduced to village aristocrats, all became political non-entities on forced migration to poor lands and continuous subjugation for 800 years from 200 BC - 600 AD under Saka-Kushan-Gurjara rule. Political decline and fall from owners of land as Kshatriya to profession of farming caused economic and educational backwardness.

Inbreeding, poor soil and wet climate deteriorated the stock; where chiefs and elite families often trans located and merged with ruling or conquering tribes. Defeats, persecution, division and absorption led to further problems.

Clans split, joining as Rajputs and Jats under new name or old names. Converts to Islam amongst the Sainis were unheard of, causing further decline as they received no favors from Turko-Pathan kings during 800 years of their rule.

In Haryana, Sainis are concentrated in the Kurukshetra, Ambala and Yamunanagar districts and are a major farming community.

Meos

Meos inhabits a territorial region that falls between the important urban centres of Delhi, Agra and Jaipur. Mewat, consisting of some adjoining parts of Haryana, Rajasthan and Uttar Pradesh, where the Meos have lived for a millennium, was a terrain of peasant radicalism in the pre-independence period. It saw intensive work by the communist leaders such as the historian-activist Kunwar Muhammad Ashraf and others then working with the Indian National Congress. There was a close inter community relationship between the Meos and other peasant-pastoral castes such as the Jats, the Ahirs and the Gujars. In Haryana the Mewat region falls in the districts of Gurgaon and Faridabad.

Meo men are tall and dark, with ponderous turbans woven around their heads, dressed in long flowing robes. The Meos are about a million-strong tribe, a Muslim Rajput community living in southern Haryana and north eastern Rajasthan known for its admixture of Hindu and Islamic customs, practices and beliefs. Only one in ten Meos is able to properly read and write.

The Meos have two identities, both of which they are equally proud of. On the one hand, they claim to be Muslims, tracing their conversion to various Sufi saints who began settling in their territory from the eleventh century onwards, and whose shrines or 'dargahs' today dot the entire Mewati countryside. On the other hand, they also claim to be Rajputs, and believe that they are direct descendants of Krishna and Rama. These Hindu deities are respectfully referred to by the Meos as 'dada' or grandfather'.

Almost every Meo village has a mosque, but in many places Meos also worship at Hindu temples. Many Rajasthani Meos still retain mixed Hindu-Muslim names. Names such as Ram Khan or Shankar Khan are not unusual in the Meo tracts in Alwar. The Muslim community of Meos is highly Hinduised. They celebrate Diwali and Holi as they celebrate Ids. They do not marry within ones Gotras like Hindus of the North though Islam permits marriage with cousins. Solemnization of marriage among Meos is not complete without both nikah as in Islam and circling of fire as among Hindus. People with double identities, Meos believe that they are direct descendants of Krishna and Rama even as they claim to be among the unnamed prophets of God referred to in the Holy Quran.

Who is a Meo? Try and insult the Pandun Ka Kara before the Meos, see the angry result and you will get the answer. The Meo version of the Mahabharata called the Pandun Ka Kara, is performed by Mirasis or Jogis to an audience comprised of Meo Muslims, as also non-Meos. The authors, performers and audience are, thus, all Muslim. The Meos regards the Mahabharata clans as the ancestors of their own lineage.

The folk epic then is far more than mere "myth" and is central to the cultural identity of the Meo Muslims. It is important to understand what the great epic means to them, how they remake, modify and recreate it and also how in the process they draw upon, modify and critique the so-called "great tradition" of Vedic and Puranic Hinduism.

Muslim musicians, called Mirasis, dressed in flowing white Kurtas and dhotis and bright crimson turbans. They play a musical rendering of the 'Pandun Ke Kara', the Meo Muslim version of the famous Hindu epic, the Mahabharata, after a brief ode in praise of the Prophet Muhammad and the Sufi saint Khwaja Moinuddin Chishti of Ajmer.

The entire epic in its Meo form, rendered in the Mewati dialect, consists of some 800 verses or 'dohas', and takes more than three hours to recite. It relates the story of the five Pandava brothers, whom it describes as ancestors of the Meos. Finally, it ends with verses in praise of its composer, an early eighteenth century Meo Muslim called Sadullah Khan. 'Pandun Ke Kada' is the only Muslim form of the Mahabharata that exists. Sadullah Khan is regarded by the Meos as their 'national poet' ('qaumi shair'). Today, barring a few Mirasis, no one else can recite the Pandun Ke Kada.

Aggarwals

Aggarwals claim themselves to be the followers of Maharaja Agarsen, the King of Agroha. Agroha is located about 20 Km's North-West of the City of Hissar in the State of Haryana in India and was once a very prosperous city. However, it has changed a lot due to the ravages of time.

The present day Agroha village is about 2.5 kms from the Agroha Mound, the remains of the old Agroha City. Maharaja

Agrasen proceeded to conduct 18 Maha Yagnas. He divided his kingdom among his 18 children and established the 18 gotras after the guru's of each of his children. These were: Garg, Mangal, Goyal, Kucchal, Goyan, Bansal, Kansal, Singhal, Jindal, Thingal, Airan, Dharan, Madhukul, Bindal, Mittal, Tayal, Bhandal, and Naagal.

The neighbouring kings were envious of Agroha because of its prosperity, thus they frequently attacked it. Because of these aggressions, Agroha faced numerous plights. In due course, the strength of Agroha was sapped. A huge fire engulfed the city causing the citizens to flee and disperse into various areas of Bharat. Today, these people are known as Aggarwals, Guptas or Banias. They still have the same 18 gotras that were given to them by their gurus and they carry on the fame of Maharaja Agrasen.

As per Maharaja Agrasen's guidance, the Aggarwals are in the forefront of social service. An Agroha temple Complex and Agroha Medical College are being built near Agroha (Hissar), with generous donations from whole of the Aggarwal community. Aggarwals are the top business and trading community in Haryana today.

RELIGION OF HARYANA

The majority of people in Haryana follow Hinduism and observe traditional Hindu beliefs. The people of Haryana consider themselves to be the descendants of the Aryans and Haryana as the inaugural site of the Aryan's experimentation of an agrarian society. The main gods worshipped are Shiva, Vishnu, Rama, Krishna, Hanuman and Kali, apart from others. Most of the temples are built for Vishnu and Shiva, with the former being more popular as Rama and Narayan.

Haryana was a part of Punjab till 1966, and so was home to the Sikh Gurus and a part of the Sikh empire founded by Maharaja Ranjit Singh. With the passage of time, the Jats and Sikhs intermingled and gave birth to the Jat Sikh clan, which is a more urbanised and enterprising than the simplistic Punjab Sikhs. Today, the largest concentration of Sikhs is in the northern district of Ambala.

Muslims make up about 5% of the total population. Although Islam does not preach casteism, there are three categories of Muslims in Haryana. The 'Asharf' or 'Sharaf' (noble) form the higher caste, and the 'Ajlaf' (base or mean) is the middle with 'Arzal' (lowest of all) coming at the end. There are Muslim Rajputs as well as converted Muslims. Christians, Jains and Buddhists are few and scattered across the state, while Sikhs are in large numbers in central and west Haryana.

9

Art, Architecture, Fair and Festivals

HARYANA ARTS AND CRAFTS

Haryana Arts and Crafts include a variety of style and flair. These works of art reflect the rich cultural heritage of Haryana. The famous Haryana Arts and Crafts are known all over the country for their splendid aesthetic values.

Haryana Arts and Crafts mainly include Pottery, Embroidery and Weaving, Phulkari, Chope, Durries Bagh and Paintings. Most of these are essentially village handicrafts. The Villages of Haryana are most famous for their woven works. The Haryana Shawl, an offshoot of the Kashmiri style of work, is a magnificent piece of art. Bright and brilliant colors form an essential part of the Arts and Crafts of Haryana.

The pots made in the villages of Haryana are brightly painted and designed intricately. This makes them appear very attractive. While the men make the earthen article the patterns on them are generally painted by some woman member of the family. Phulkari of Haryana is essentially a rural craft and in made by the women members. The Bagh is a bit different from the Phulkari and in this case the base cloth is completely covered with embroidery. Another kind of shawl made by the people here is the Chope.

Haryana Arts and Crafts are one of the major mode of income for the rural people of the state. Thus they play an important role in governing the economy of the state of Haryana.

Pottery

Pottery is one of the most popular occupations in the rural parts of Haryana. Since the state mainly has a rural economy so this popular form of craft is considered with much importance in Haryana. The unique feature of the earthenwares of this state is that they are painted with rich and bright colors.

Pottery involves a main potter and a helper who will help him to prepare the mix. These works are generally done by the men of the village. After these earthenwares are given shape, bright and colorful patterns are painted on them. This work is generally done by a female member of the potter's family. Thus Pottery in Haryana involves a collective effort of many people.

Pottery is popular in many corners of India. The origin of the potter's wheel can be traced back to the pre-Aryan days. They are of different kinds and shapes. The Kick- operated type is popularly used in the villages of Haryana. In this case the potter needs not use his hand for the work rather they use their foot to turn the wheels. But the hand operated wheels are more common in the other parts of the country. The wheel is made of either cement or stone.

Embroidery and Weaving

Haryana is famous for its Handlooms, Embroidery and Weaving. The shawls, lungis and Durries are the most popular among them. The Haryana Shawl known as Phulkari is appreciated all over the world for its rich Embroidery. Though it is very similar to the Kashimiri style but the Phulkari of Haryana is unique in its use of colors and patterns.

The Phulkaris are worn by the women of Haryana with their Ghagra and Choli during the winters. Another type of shawl very similar to the Phulkaris is the Bagh. Intricate embroidery is the main feature of this branch of Handlooms. Almost the entire base cloth is covered with embroidery in the Bagh styled shawls.

Phulkari and Bagh are essentially products from the rural parts of the state of Haryana. Phulkari is done by the women population of some of the villages and it generally take years to complete one such piece. Weaving starts after the birth of a girl in the family and its completed to be given as a wedding present to her.

Arts and Crafts

Haryana mainly has a rural economy and Pottery is one of the main occupation. The potter's wheel, dating back to pre-Aryan times, is the most common feature of any village in India. Although numerous kinds of wheels are used throughout India, in Haryana the kick-operated type is common. With this contraption you don't use your hands to turn the wheel as in normal cases, on the other hand, you use your foot. The actual wheel may be either of cement or stone. Pottery is essentially a village craft, and Haryana is essentially a rural state. While the potter works on the wheel, he has a helper (usually his son or a relative) mixing clay, while a woman (his wife or a sister) makes intricate designs into the finished vessel or toy. From utensils to toys to decorative pieces, clay forms the most essential ingredient on which the potter literally survives. Seasonal festivals call for the potter to get cracking – he has to make hundreds of toys like miniature cows, horses, people, houses and sepoys which are then sold in brightly decorated stalls along dusty lanes.

Embroidery, Weaving and Handlooms: Haryana is quite famous for its woven work, be it shawls, durries, robes or lungis. The Haryana shawl is known as "Phulkari". It is an offshoot of the shawl from Kashmir. It is a spectacular piece of clothing, full of magnificent colours and intricate embroidery. Worn with a tightfitting choli (blouse) and Ghagra (long skirt), it forms the basic winter wear for the women of Haryana. A deviation from the phulakri is the "bagh" (garden).

In this case, the entire cloth is covered with embroidery. The phulkari is made by female members of a house, and takes a long time to make; sometimes even a few years. Traditionally, work on a phulkari commences from the time a daughter is born in the family and is given to her at her wedding. Against a red background, motifs of birds, flowers and human figures are stitched into the cloth.

The bagh design almost always follows a geometric pattern, with green as the basic colour probably because mainly Muslims worked on them. Although lacking in technical finesse, it makes up for the loss by a colourful display of its design.

Haryana durries are rather coarse, although spectacular geometric designs adorn the entire rug. The durries made with white triangles often set against a blue background are quite popular. In Haryana, durrie making is concentrated in and around Panipat.

PAINTING

Haryana was always a rendezvous for various tribes, invaders, races, cultures and faiths, going right back to BC 2500, and it witnessed the merging of numerous styles of painting. Discoveries of earthenware and designs painted on them in black and white found Siswal site, are the first impressions of art in this state. Mitathal and Banawali sites have also revealed that art did exist here, but definitely on a much smaller scale than that of the Deccan and southern India. The drawings are mainly in horizontal and vertical lines, with a little more creativity allotted to floral art. During Harshvardhana's reign art and painting received special attention for some time as the king himself was a painter of sorts.

In the past, the rich jagirdars (landlords) who liked paintings engaged artisans and painters to do up their houses; ceilings and the walls. Temples were another area where the painter got to work, decorating everything within reach with landscapes, dances, hunting expeditions, wrestling bouts, birds, bees, and love scenes. Come the 18th century, and the Marwaris made sure that painters got enough work, albeit under a Rajput style. The god Krishna was a big hit in the villages - walls, doors, windows all bore his likeness with the Mughal and Kangra styles merging with the Rajput style.

The walls of the palace of Maharaja Tej Singh in Mirpur in Gurgaon is adorned with paintings, following the Rajput pattern. The patterns on the walls express scenes from the Ramayana. The Asthal Bohar paintings are also in the Rajput style, and their influence can be seen even in the Shiva temples in Panchkula and Pinjore, Venumadhava temple in Kaul, the temples in Kaithal and Pabnama, the Kapil temple in Kilayat and the Sarsainth temple in Sirsa. The Rang Mahal in Pinjore is also decorated with wall paintings, an originality straight from the hands of Mughal painters. The samadhis of Lala Balk Ram and Lala Jamuna Das in Jagadhari in Ambala are famous for their wall paintings from Hindu mythology. The entrances to both are flanked by heavily painted dwarapalas.

Kurukshetra's Bhadri Kali temple has religious themes and frescos running throughout its structure. The second floor is covered with murals, as is the haveli (house) of Rani Chand Kaur in Pehowa, the temple of Shri Ram Radha in Pehowa and the temple of Baba Shrawan Nath. In fact, you'll find similar paintings in temples and holy Hindu places throughout Haryana.

The Persian style infused with script also gains prominence, especially with murals in which the Persian script is freely used. Mughal paintings also seeped into Hindu temples, especially in Kaithal, Kalayat and Rohtak. In Rohtak paintings have been found which are now in possession of the Manuscripts Department of Kurukshetra University. Liberal use of blue, pink, green, orange and red enhance the beauty of these paintings, which are of the Lord Vishnu and his incarnations.

Sculpture: Sculpture Rock and stone were the most common subjects for the development of art, right from the Maurya period to Harshvardhan to the Mughals and the British. Gods formed the basis of sculpture in ancient Haryana, and likewise all over India. Sculpture in Haryana was concentrated around central and northern parts and was basically religious in content. Vishnu was the most important, and he and his incarnations were enough material for sculptors to start cutting away.

A figure of Vishnu found in Kurukshetra is a remarkable piece of art, showing the god with four arms gracefully reclining on the coils of Anantnag, the many-headed snake.

This stone figure was probably made in the 10th century AD. Sandstone was widely used, be it green, buff, gray or black. But besides the images of Hindu gods and goddesses, Jain images from the Pratihara period (9th century) have also been found, all made of sandstone.

The Buddha also surfaces once in a while, like in Rohtak where he was found seated cross-legged on a lotus pedestal and made entirely of gray stone.

Local Sayings: The Hindi word (Kahawat) literally means a saying. It is derived from Hindi (Kahana) "to say". Haryanavi may be stated as one of the languages which gave birth to (khari boli) hindi, many of its kahawats are found in Hindi, still there are some which can be stated in pure haryanwi language. In day to day life of Haryana one can come across a lot of prose and phrases and it is difficult to note all of them. In a village at every corner where men are sitting smoking hookahs or where women are working in a field kahawats are living parts of their conversation.

An old man seeing a man becoming rich says, "Ajkal dharti pe paon na tiktey iskey". It means he is flying high, this is a kahawat. I am trying to write a few haryanawi kahawats, hope you enjoy them:

1. Kag padhaya pinjarey, padh gaya charon ved, samjhayan

samjhya nahin, rahya dhed ka dhed:

You cannot educate a crow like a parrot even if you teach him in a cage, he will not understand anything just like a foolish man will remain foolish and wont change.

2. Ghar dhek key khaye, padosi dekh kamaye: Spend according to your income and earn as your neighbor.
3. Ocha baniaa, god ka chhohra, ochhay ki preet, and baloo ki bheent, kadey sukh nahi dey: A cunning money lender, adopted son, cruel love and a sand wall will never give happiness.
4. Paon saday, ghoda aday, vidya bisar jaye, roti jaley angar pe, koh chela, kis pher? Guruji, phera nahi:

   "Burning feet, reluctant horse, forgotten knowledge, burnt bread, what's all this?" asks teacher. The pupil foolishly replies, "Dont know".
5. Mat Mari Jatki, rangarh rakhya halli, vo usney kam kahey, vo de usney galli: The Jat has acted foolishly by keeping a ranghar (notorious member of society) as his farm worker, each time he tells him to work, the ranghar retorts by abuses.
6. Jis ghar bara na maniye, dhori parey na ghas, sas bahu ka ho ladna, ujad ho jiya bas: A house where elders are not respected, cows are not fed well, where mother-in-law and daughter-in-law fight, that house can never flourish.
7. Jis ghar bara na bajhiye, diva jaley na sanjh, so ghar ujad, janiye, ja ghar tiriya banjh: In homes where elders opinions are not valued, where lamp is not lighted in the evening, where women is barren, know that house is finished.
8. Jab chinti anda le chaley, chiriya nahvey dhool main, kahey sianay sun bhai, barsay ghag jarror: When ants carry eggs, sparrows play in sand then it will rain definitely.
9. Jiski choudi ho papakhi aur patli naarh, issi bhans bisahvo yar: Whose back is broad and has a thick neck, that buffalo is best, buy it.

10. Joban lugai ka bees ya tees, ar bael chaley nou saal. mard aur ghora kadey no ho burha, agar milley khurak: Youth of a woman is 20 or 30, ox remain active till 9 years, but man and horse, if given good diet never get old.
11. Jat kahey jatni say, jay is gam main sukhi rehna. Chinti kha gi hathi nay, hanji hanji kehna: Jat says to his wife, "If you want to live happily in this state, then just say yes to every lie, even when someone says an ant has eaten an elephant.
12. Jay baniya banja hakim, to gajab khuda: If businessmen become rulers, then God only can help.
13. Bhai, bhinoi, bhanja aur bhupal in charon nay chodkar, kitey karo viyapar:

    Do not include brother, nephew, brother-in-law and other relatives in partnership, if you want to do business.
14. Tan say ujla man say sanvala, bugley jisa bhekh. Aisay te kaga bhala bahar bhitar ek: Those who are fair from outside and ill natured from inside are like Agarate. Ais better than it who is same from outside and inside in other words those who do not hide their true feelings are better.
15. Kothey upar tumadi, ke degi dumdi: One who has already hidden eatables such a miser can help no one.
16. Sanghi ka kam marey, Aur marrey bhadvay ka gham: For a farmer farming in partnership and hot summers in September are both harmful.
17. Kaya rahey nirog, jo kum khaye. uska bigdhay na kam, jo gum khaye: He who eats less remains healthy. He never fails who does not get depressed.
18. Dani kal parakhyo, gay ne phagan mah.bahu nay jas din parakhye, jab dhan palley na: He who helps in need is great, cow who gives milk even in April (in summers) is good and women is judged when there is no money.
19. Chatur hai je bairi to bhi theek, par murkh bhala na miit. keh gaye siyaney kadey na kariyu murakh jan say preet:

An enemy if wise is better than a stupid friend. Wise men say never be friends with a fool.

20. Muh lagai gar dumani, gavegi all patal: Never keep foolish person nearby, as he can say anything at any time.

The Origin Of Painting In Haryana

Haryana had been the point of confluence for various tribes, invaders, races, cultures and faiths, antedating to 2500 BC and it witnessed the merging of numerous styles of painting. Discoveries of earthenware and designs painted on them in black and white in Siswal district in Haryana are the first impressions of art in this state. Mitathal and Banwali districts have also revealed that art did exist here, but definitely on a much smaller scale than that of the Deccan and southern India. The drawings are mainly in horizontal and vertical lines, with a little more creativity allotted to floral art.

Art and painting received special attention for some time during King Harsha's reign, as the King himself was a painter and a connoisseur of arts. After Harsha's death, painting flourished for a while under the Rajputs, but the establishment of the Delhi Sultanate put an end to this. The Sultans had no love for art and were busy fighting wars and battles and never patronised art.

Art reached its epitome during the reign of Mughal Empire. Jehangir was a patron of art, and during his rule the influence of the Persian painting style was happily married to the Indian style.

In the past, the rich jagirdars (landlords) who were great patrons of art, engaged artisans and painters to do up their houses; ceilings and the walls. Temples of the region have provided the painters an arena to exhibit their work, decorating everything within reach with landscapes, dances, hunting expeditions, wrestling bouts, birds, bees and love scenes. Come the 18th century, and the Rewaris made sure that painters got enough work, albeit under a Rajput style. The mirthful god, Krishna has aroused most artistic fervours in the villages - walls, doors, and windows all bore this likeness with the Mughal and Kangra styles merging with the Rajput style.

The Art On Display

The walls of the palace of Maharaja Tej Singh in Mirpur in Gurgaon are adorned with paintings done in Rajput style. The patterns on the walls depict scenes from the Ramayana. The 'Matru Mad ki Piao' in Gurgaon features mythological paintings, but these are slowly fading away. The 'Asthal Bohar' paintings are also in the Rajput style, and their influence can be seen even in the Shiva temples in Panchkula and Pinjore, Venumadhava temple in Kaul, the temples in Kaithal and Pabnama, the Kapil temple in Kilayat and the Sarsainth temple in Sirsa.

The Rang Mahal in Pinjore is also decorated with wall paintings, an originality straight from the hands of Mughal painters.

The 'samadhis' of Lala Balak Ram and Lala Jamuna Das in Jagadhari in Ambala are famous for their wall paintings from Hindu mythology. The entrances to both are flanked by heavily painted 'dwarapalas'. The Rajiwala temple near the 'samadhis' also boasts of religious themes in its paintings. Its walls, cells and verandah have been subjected to the Jain style, while the Qila Mubarak, a two-storeyed Mughal structure is embellished with images of birds and flowers.

Kurukshetra's Bhadra Kali temple has religious themes and frescoes running throughout its structure, with a broad frieze bordering the lower end. The second storey is covered with murals, as is the haveli (house) of Rani Chand Kaur and the temple of Shri Ram Radha in Pehowa and the temple of Baba Shrawan Nath. There are similar paintings in temples and holy Hindu places throughout Haryana.

The Elaborate Use of Calligraphy

The Persian style infused with script also gained prominence, especially with murals in which the Persian script is freely used. Elaborate details form the central theme within which verses from the Quran are written in various flowing styles, following the calligraphy method.

Mughal paintings also seeped into Hindu temples, especially in Kaithal, Kalayat and Rohtak. Here too, the subject matter has been heavily inspired by mythology and carries moral and spiritual messages. In Rohtak, paintings have been found, which are now in possession of the Manuscripts Department of Kurukshetra University. Liberal use of blue, pink, green, orange and red enhance the beauty of these paintings, which basically depict Lord Vishnu and his incarnations.

FAIRS

Along with the mesmerising architecture and numerous tourist attractions, Haryana has gained a lot of fame for the lively fairs organised there. The most acclaimed of these are-

Surajkund International Fair

This fair set up in the suburbs of Faridabad every year is a heaven for craft and handloom lovers.

With the splash of colours and the rhythm of the drum beats, this fair beautifully portrays the rural part of their culture and is a super success every year. Adorned with multicuisine food courts and different adventure and amusement rides, this mela is attended by thousands of people from nearby places.

Baisakhi Mela

Hosted by the Haryana Tourism on 13-14th April at Pinjore Gardens every year, this fair commemorates the festival of Baisakhi. A plethora of visitors witness the celebrations with great enthusiasm and frolic.

Pinjore Heritage Festival

This festival is celebrated every year in the month of December to celebrate the vibrant and rich culture of Haryana. Poets, singers and dancers perform their art forms here. This is a great annual event that focuses on the history and heritage of old Pinjore town and its magnificent gardens.

Mango Mela

Organized in the months of June and July at 'Yadavindra Gardens' of Pinjore, this mela is a great treat for the mango lovers.

The Mango Mela does not only quenches the people's desires o the different variety of mangoes but also offers a forum to support the farmers to sell their mangoes and teach them about the latest technology to raise their mango production.

FESTIVALS

To celebrate various occasions and events, a number of vibrant festivals take place in Haryana. These festivals include Teej, Guga Navmi, Gita Jayanti, Kaartik Cultural Festival and a unique celebration known as Sohna Car Rally. The most famous festival of all times is Teej. It is usually celebrated on the third day of 'Shrawana' month. The festival is celebrated with great pomp and enthusiasm all over the state. Swings are set up in the gardens and the girls apply henna on their hands. Young Girls and women get dressed up in colourful and vibrant clothes and engage in dancing and singing throughout the evening.

Fairs and Festivals in Haryana

The state of Haryana celebrates the rich, glorious culture of India in its various fairs and festivals that are celebrated with equal pomp and gaiety here as all over the country. There are several fairs and festivals in Haryana that attract a large number of visitors to the state at different times of the year. These festivals are occasions of celebration, fun and frolic when the entire state of Haryana bustles with life.

Perhaps the major and most popular fair in Haryana is the Surajkund Crafts Mela that is held in the month of February. The fortnight-long fair takes place every year from 1st - 15th February. The event provides one of the best platforms to local artisans and craftsmen from all over India to showcase their products to a large audience that arrives to witness this important annual event. Surajkund Crafts Mela is truly the largest exhibition of local crafts in India that allows numerous talented craftsmen in the country to bring to the fore their unique hand-made products and offerings. Make sure to visit the fair during your tour to Haryana.

Some of the other important fairs and festivals in Haryana that are celebrated in the state with much fervor are Lohri (13th January), Baisakhi (13th April), Teej, Sanjhi (October), Kurukshetra Festival in Haryana (May-June), Kurukshetra Festival in Kurukshetra (Nov-Dec) and Mango Festival (May-June).

FAIRS AND FESTIVALS

Gangore is celebrated on Chet Sudi-3 (Mar-Apr). Idols of Ishar and Gangore are taken out in procession and songs in their praise are sung till they are immersed into water. This spring festival is held in honour of Gauri, the goddess of abundance. Girls dress up in their finest clothes and pray for a spouse of their choice, while married ladies do the same for the happiness of their husbands. Girls worship the goddess throughout the preceding fortnight. Colourful images of Gauri, beautifully dressed and bejeweled, are taken out in procession with the town band. Thousands of people take part in the procession of the Gangore image from village to village.

Teej is celebrated on Sawan Sudi - 3 (Jul-Aug). It is celebrated to welcome 'Sawan' or the rainy season. After first showers of Sawan, a small red insect called Teej in Haryana comes out from earth's soil. Swings are set up in the open courtyards and Teej gets the first swing of the season. Girls apply henna on their hands and feet and are excused from household chores on this day. On Teej girls receive new clothes from their parents and the mother sends a baya or gift. Puja is performed in the morning. The baya which consists of a variety of foodstuff is placed on a thali at the place of worship where a chowk (square) has been decorated, an idol or a picture of Parvati is installed. The evenings are set aside for singing and dancing.

Janamashtami is celebrated as the birth anniversary of Krishna, the incarnation of Lord Vishnu. The temples witness an extravagant and colourful celebration on this occasion. Raslila is performed to recreate incidents from the life of Krishna and to commemorate his love for Radha. The image of the infant Krishna is bathed at midnight and is placed in a cradle. Devotional songs and dances mark the celebration of this festive occasion all over Northern India. This festival is celebrated with a special fervour by people of 'Brij Bhoomi' area of Faridabad district.

Diwali or Deepawali is a festival of lights symbolizing the victory of righteousness and the lifting of spiritual darkness. The word 'Deepawali' literally means rows of 'deepaks' or 'diyas' (clay lamps). It is celebrated 20 days after Dusshera on the 13th day of the dark fortnight of the month of Asvin (Oct-Nov). Continuing the story of Ram, this festival commemorates Lord Ram's return to his kingdom Ayodhya after completing his 14-year exile. Twinkling diyas and candles light up every home and firework displays are common all across the country.

The goddess Lakshmi, who is the symbol of wealth and prosperity, is also worshipped on this day. Lord Ganesh, the symbol of auspiciousness and wisdom, is also worshipped in most Hindu homes on this day. The occasion of Diwali sees the spring-cleaning and white-washing of houses; decorative designs or *rangolis* are painted on floors and walls. New clothes are bought and family members and relatives gather together to offer prayers, distribute sweets and to light up their homes.

Holi is a spring festival. It is celebrated in the month of Phalgun, as the lunar month is locally known. The main event of Holi is indeed a carnival of colours. On this day, children, friends and neighbours come out on the streets. And the spree to colour-anyone-you-see takes over. Colours of all form and variety. They come in shades of red, orange, blue, green and purple, and the likes. Coloured powder, or, gulal was earlier made out of Dried seeds of some tropical flowers like the Palash, and dried silt from the river bed. This has now given way to dyes, available in the form of pigments.

People throw these coloured powders in the air as they shout "Holi Hai!" and smear each other with this coloured powder. Also they wet each other with coloured water from Pitchkaris, a type of water gun. Coloured water is prepared by mixing the pigments of dyes. These dyes are available in a range of shades. Also water-filled balloons are used these days to charge the target with a splash of colour.

Dusshera is one of the important Hindu festivals, celebrated with much fervour in the entire country. The occasion marks the triumph of Lord Ram over the demon king, Ravan, the victory of good over evil. Brilliantly decorated tableaux and processions depicting various facets of Ram's life are taken out.

On the tenth day, the Vijayadasmi day, huge effigies of Ravan, his brother Kumbhkaran and son Meghnath are placed in open spaces. Ram, accompanied by his consort Sita and his brother Lakshman, arrive and shoot arrows of fire at these effigies, which are stuffed with explosive material. The result is a deafening blast, enhanced by the shouts of merriment and triumph from the spectators. In burning the effigies the people are asked to burn the evil within them, and thus follow the path of virtue and goodness, bearing in mind the instance of Ravan, who despite all his might and majesty was destroyed for his evil ways.

Lohri marks the culmination of winter, and is celebrated on the 13 Jan a day before Makar Sankranti. For Punjabis, this is an important festival. Lohri celebrates fertility and the spark of life. People gather round the bonfires, throw sweets, puffed rice and popcorn into the flames, sing songs and exchange greetings.

The prasad comprises of things like til, gazak, gur, moongphali, phuliya and popcorn. There is puja, involving parikrama around the fire and distribution of prasad. This symbolizes a prayer to Agni, the spark of life, for abundant crops and prosperity. The first Lohri of a bride is extremely important. The first Lohri of a newborn baby, whether a girl or a boy, is also equally important. Children go from door to door singing and asking for the Lohri prasad.

Basant Panchami celebrated Haryana, Delhi and Punjab, to welcome spring season, held in Feb-Mar. Main event: Kite flying Baisakhi celebrated with joyous music and dancing, is New Year's Day for Punjabis. It falls on April 13, though once in 36 years it occurs on 14th April. It was on this day that the tenth Sikh Guru, Guru Gobind Singh, founded the Khalsa in 1699. Sikhs visits *Gurdwaras* and listen to kirtans. After the prayer, *kada prasad* (sweetened semolina) is served to the congregation.

The function ends with *langar*, the community lunch. Processions are taken out, at the head of which are the *panj piaras*. Mock duels and bands playing religious tunes are part of the processions. School children also enthusiastically take part in them. For people in villages this festival is a last opportunity for relaxing before they start harvesting of corn. Processions and feasting follow readings of the holy scripture of the Sikhs, Guru Granth Sahib.

Guggapir is celebrated on the next day of Janamashtami. Gugga Pir is worshipped by both Hindus and Muslims. A dance procession is taken out in which Panch Pirs are the main dancers. They sing songs in praise of Gugga.

Mansa Devi Mela is held in Bilaspur village near of Mani Majra (Chandigarh). There are two temples dedicated to the goddess here. The fairs are held twice a year in March-April (Chat shudiashtami) and September-October (asoj shudi ashtami).

Chetar Chaudas Mela is annually held in Pehowa, which has the holy Saraswati tank also called 'Saraswati Teertha' or

'Prithudak Teertha'. This Teertha also finds mention in the ancient Hindu texts. Here in this place the Chetar Chaudas Fair is held in the spring season. Pilgrims, both Sikhs and Hindus, flock to this place to offer 'pinds' for their ancestors. It is claimed that here in this holy spot, Yudhister had offered 'pinds' in memory of all their relatives killed in the Mahabharat war. Pilgrims take bath in the Saraswati tank during this fair.

Sili Sate fair is held to worship Sitamata.

Nirjala Akadshi is in the month of Jaishth. The women keep fast and abstain from water.

Madlia Naumi is celebrated at the beginning of the rainy season.

Sanjhi is celebrated for 10 days in the month of Asuj. Sarka Devi is mainly worshipped in these days.

SURAJ KUND CRAFTS MELA

The very first effort on organizing cultural events on a national level by Haryana Tourism was done with the launching of the annual and now internationally famous Surajkund Crafts Mela, that began in 1981. The Crafts Mela celebrates the finest handlooms and handicrafts traditions of country. It is a fortnight long event that embodies the spirit that runs through the people of India and its rich culture. It is held in the month of February from 1st-15th. The Surajkund Crafts Mela is held just 8 km from south Delhi.

Beneath thatched roof platforms, master crafts persons carefully display the finest of handlooms and handicrafts from all over the country. The event is so colourful and rich in experience, that many a tourist has returned to visit it again and again.

The prices are relatively low compared to emporia, and some of the stuff can be amazing. Shops at the Mela bustle with the brilliance of mirror encasing embroidery, delicate lace work, folk motifs on terracotta forms, metal and cane-ware, the tinkle of bangles, shimmer of iridescent silks and the jingle of toys and trinkets. The Surajkund Crafts Mela is more than a celebration of crafts. At the fan shaped open-air-theatre name 'Natyashala' rich folk dances and musical evenings are held throughout the mela fortnight.

How to reach Surajkund: Surajkund lies in the Faridabad district on the Delhi - Agra national highway. Surajkund is 8 kms from South Delhi. Special transport link the Mela ground to major bus stops in Delhi, Gurgaon and Faridabad towns.

The Mela begins from 9.30 a.m. and closes at 5.30 p.m. each evening from 1st to 15th February every year.

The Kartik Fair: The Kartik Cultural Festival of Haryana is the result of the consolidated effort of Haryana Tourism working with a number of allied agencies. Prominent among those were the Ministry of Tourism and Department of Culture, Government of India, Department of Youth Affairs and Sports, Govt. of India, Department of Cultural Affairs, Haryana, Development Commissioners Handlooms and Handicrafts, North Zone Cultural Centre, North Central Cultural Centre, Nehru Yuva Kendra Sangathan and Ballabhgarh Development and Beautification Society.

The very first effort on organizing cultural events on a national level by Haryana Tourism was done with the launching of the annual and now internationally famous Surajkund Crafts Mela, that began in 1981. Whereas the Crafts Mela celebrates the finest handlooms and handicrafts traditions of country, the Kartik Cultural Festival was planned with the express view of promoting fort ambience, martial arts and the rich repertoire of both classical Indian music and dance, matching it with an equally rich variety of folk theatre. The festival had given new life to dying folk arts, martial arts and worked to bring traditional folk dances and music to the national stage.

The Kartik Cultural Festival was held at the Nahar Singh Mahal that lies in Ballabhgarh town. The fort, the venue of the festival was built by the forefathers of Raja Nahar Singh around 1739 A.D. Raja Nahar Singh after whom the palace is named ascended the throne in 1829 A.D. The Raja was a young king of the empire of the last Mughal Emperor Bahadur Shah Zaffar. He gave up his life fighting for the cause of the ruler in the country's First War of Independence in 1847.

The palace of Nahar Singh was identified for beautification by the Government of Haryana and restored to its original glory by a well known team of experts of Francis Nacziarg and Aman Nath who worked on many such restoration projects. The Mahal is an outstanding specimen of architectural design. The Palace was decorated with an elaborate cupola and minars. In pattern, the palace carries a reflection of the finesse of the mahals of Bharatpur.

10

Education

INTRODUCTION

During 2001-02, there were 11, 013 primary schools, 1, 918 middle schools, 3, 023 high schools and 1, 301 senior secondary schools in the state. Haryana Board of School Education, established in September 1969 and shifted to Bhiwani in 1981, conducts public examinations at middle, matriculation, and senior secondary levels twice a year. Over seven lakh candidates attend annual examinations in February and March, and 150, 000 attend supplementary examinations each November. The Board also conducts examinations for Haryana Open School at senior and senior secondary levels twice a year. The Haryana government provides free education to women up to graduation level.

Maharaja Agrasen Institute of Medical Research & Education, Agroha (Hisar district)

There are four universities in the state. Technical education and management studies are provided by Maharshi Dayanand University at Rohtak, Kurukshetra University at Kurukshetra and Guru Jambheshwar University at Hisar. Chaudhary Charan Singh Haryana Agricultural University at Hisar is one of the biggest agricultural universities in Asia. It is engaged in education, research and development related to agriculture. The National Dairy Research Institute at Karnal provides education in the field of dairy science. It has been upgraded to the level of a Deemed University. There are medical colleges in Rohtak and Agroha.

Drawbacks: The schooling network in villages is inadequate with the ever growing population. Also the education system suffers from corruption and inefficiency.

Pt. B.D. Sharma PGIMS Rohtak

Literacy

Literacy rate in Haryana has seen an upward trend and is 76.64 percent as per 2011 population census. Male literacy stands at 85.38 percent, while female literacy is at 66.67 percent. In 2001, the literacy rate in Haryana stood at 67.91 percent of which male and female were 78.49 percent and 55.73 percent literate respectively. As of 2013, Gurgaon city had the highest literacy rate in Haryana at 86.30% followed by Panchkula at 81.9 per cent and Ambala at 81.7 percent. In terms of districts, as of 2012 Rewari had the highest literacy rate in Haryana at 74%, higher than the national average of 59.5%: male literacy was 79%, and female 67%.

Schools

Haryana Board of School Education, established in September 1969 and shifted to Bhiwani in 1981, conducts public examinations at middle, matriculation, and senior secondary levels twice a year. Over seven lakh candidates attend annual examinations in February and March; 150,000 attend supplementary examinations each November. The Board also conducts examinations for Haryana Open School at senior and senior secondary levels twice a year. The Haryana government provides free education to women up to the bachelor's degree level.

In 2015-2016, there were nearly 20,000 schools, including 10,100 state government schools (36 Aarohi Schools, 11 Kasturba Gandhi Balika Vidyalayas, 21 Model Sanskriti Schools, 8744 government primary school, 3386 government middle school, 1284 government high school and 1967 government senior secondary schools), 7,635 private schools (200 aided, 6612 recognized unaided, and 821 unrecognied unaided private schools.)and several hundred other central government and private schools such as Kendriya Vidyalaya, Indian Army Public Schools, Jawahar Navodaya Vidyalaya and DAV schools affiliated to central government's CBSE and ICSE school boards.

BOARD OF SCHOOL EDUCATION

Activities and Achievements: The Board of School Education Haryana was set up in September, 1969 with its headquarters at Chandigarh. The Board started with a staff of 100 officials alocated from Punjab University, Chandigarh in the year 1969 and conducted first Matric Examination in 1970 and 79,970 candidates had appeared in this examination. The number of candidates now has increased to 3,20,000 in 2001. The Board conducted Middle Examination with effect from 1976 to improve educational standard at middle level and 1,06,507 candidates and appeared in this examination. The candidates has now increased to 3,000 in 2001.

The Headquarters, of the Board was shifted to Bhiwani on January 12, 1981 and the administrative Block of the Board named Dr. Radhakrishanan Bhawan was inaugurated on January 13,986. At present 786 employees and officers are working in the Board which has 36 Branches and Cells. The Board set up in-house computer in the year 1986 for computerization of all the work of the Board.

The Board adopted 10+2 pattern of education and conduct of XII class examination under the new scheme with effect from 1987 in which 35215 candidates had appeared. The number of candidates has now increased to 1,96,000 in 2001. It started conducting 10+2 Vocational Examination in 1990 keeping in view the vocationalisation of education and the fast changing economic scenario.

The main function of the Board of School Education Haryana is to conduct Public Examinations at Middle, Matric, and Sr. Sec. (Academic & Vocational) levels twice a year. The Board also conducts examinations of open learning system named Haryana Open School at Secondary & Senior Secondary levels twice a year.

Besides the main function of the conducting examinations, the board also take effective steps for educational improvement. Thus the long term goal of the Board is to raise the standard of Education in the State by bringing quality improvement in it. It is sincerely felt that the Board is not nearly an examining body, hence the scope of activity of the Board is enlarged to encompass improvement in the School Education.

Keeping in view the above ideas, the Board initiated various innovations in the field of education in the state beginning fro launching of Anti-coping Campaign to establishing Haryana Open School for Universalisation of Education, granting affiliation to schools to schools to ensure better infrastructural facilities and proper academic atmosphere, starting the enrolment scheme of students to eleminate mall practices like Bogus admission; organising seminars Workshops and orientation programmes for teachers improving the techniques of paper setting and evaluation; modifying curriculum to suit the needs and aspirants of the students of Haryana; to include moral education as a compulsory subject upto Senior Secondary

Level etc. The Anti-coping Campaign brought a revolutionary change in the field of education in Haryana. It is changed the psyche of the people and students and made them understand the futility and immorality of the evil practice of copying. The Campaign helped in restoration of people's faith in the sanctity of examinations.

The practice of mass-copying and outside disturbance were checked to a considerable extent. The teachers started teaching and the students started studying sincerely. The turn out of teachers on examinations duty increased considerably and they started performing their duties with dedication, zeal and sincerity. Besides the Anti-Copying Campaign the Board is seriously working towards bringing qualitative improvement in school education so that quality human resources can be developed for the state and the country.

BOARD OF SCHOOL EDUCATION HARYANA, BHIWANI

Various Branches

Introduction: The Board of School Education Haryana with its Headquarters at Bhiwani was set up in September, 1969 to bring about qualitative improvement in School Education and conduct of copying-free examination in the vast interest of all the stockholders. The overall aim of the Board is to provide the right kind of education in the best possible way. The conduct of examination is just one of the facets of the working of the Board and the whole endeavour is geared to improve the standard of education in all its dimensions.

The Board provides the following services through its various branches:

Academic/Education Wing

This Branch undertakes all academic matters like designing the curriculum, development of text books, framing academic as well as examination rules & regulations, getting matters of equivalence of various examinations decided, organize seminars, workshops etc. for teachers and other personnel.

In a nutshell, this Branch is responsible not only for maintaining standards & quality in education but also for planning action for educational improvement in the State.

Various Committees like the Academic Affairs Committee, Subject Committees, Equivalence Committee, Editorial Committee etc. where academicians are involved are constituted and meetings of these committees are convened by this Branch. There is a rich library in the Board containing 35, 000 books on various topics.

Enrolment Branch

The Board of School Education Haryana has decided to start Enrolment of students from class VIIIth instead of IXth from Annual Examinations-2004.

All regular and private candidates would be enrolled from class VIIIth from Annual Examinations-2004 the fees of which had been Rs.20/- for each candidate as per the existing practice. The fee would have to be deposited with the Examination fee.

The Board would send Enrolment forms with details along with the certificates of pass candidates of Middle. If a candidate fails in class VIIIth, he/she would have to apply for enrolment again with a prescribed fee of Rs.20/-. The earlier Enrolment return of such candidates would stand cancelled.

The enrolment number issued to candidates would remain the same up to Senior Secondary Class.

By starting enrolment from class VIIIth, only cases of students from other States/Boards who take admission in the schools affiliated to the Board of School Education Haryana of class nine, ten, eleven and twelve will remain. Thus the Board would get the T.C. and S.L.C. of such students checked and then issue them enrolment numbers. The new system will facilitate hundred percent checking of students from other Boards/States.

After the prescribed dates are over, the Supplementary Enrolment Returns of that year can be sent with a late fee of Rs.500/- only after the approval of the Secretary, Board.

The record of the concerned schools would be checked and if an institution does not submit the required documents up to fifteen days before the commencement of Examinations, The Board would cancel the enrolment numbers of the students of such institutions for which the concerned institutions/ students would be solely responsible.

The last date of submitting Enrolment Returns with late fee has been fixed December 31 of every year by the Board of School Education Haryana and after this date no return will be acceptable under any circumstances.

Enrolment Dates for IXth, Xth, XIth & XIIth classes are as follows:

	Without late fee	*With late fee*
IXth	15.10.2004	With Rs.500/- late fee forms
Xth	30.9.2004	will be accepted till 31.12.2004
XIth		30.9.2004 With permission from the
XIIth	30.9.2004	Secretary.

Examination Branches (Middle, Matric & Senior Secondary)

These Branches are responsible for receiving and processing the Examination Forms of their respective classes (Middle, Matric or Sr.Sec.)

After bringing modification in the rules and regulations of Middle, Matric and Senior Secondary (Academic and Vocational) Examinations, the Board has decided to allow candidates to change their subject one month before the commencement of Examinations and for this the fee has been reduced to Rs.100/

- from Rs. 200/-.

The Examination forms of private candidates of Annual Examinations February/ March-2004 to be conducted by the Board of School Education, Haryana will not be accepted in any case after the prescribed last dates.

The private candidates of Middle Annual Examination could submit their forms with a late fee of Rs.300/- up to January 2, 2004. The private candidates of Matric and Senior Secondary Certificate Examination could submit their forms with late fee of Rs.300/- up to January 13, 2004. No form would be accepted after these dates since the Board has dispensed with the provision of submitting Examination forms with a late fee of Rs.500/- and Rs.1000/-.

The candidates, who want to change their subject because of error in their examination forms, could apply for the same with a prescribed fee of Rs.100/- up to December 31, 2003. This date would not be extended and no application would be accepted in this regard.

CONDUCT BRANCH

This Branch is responsible for planning and actually conducting the Board Examinations. It is responsible for finalizing the examination centres, assigning centres to students/ examinees, appointing Centre Superintendents, supervisory staff as well as various kinds of Flying Squads.

The Board has announced the dates of Middle, Matric and Senior Secondary (Academic and Vocational) Annual and Supplementary Examinations-2004 and that of Haryana Open School. The Middle Annual Examinations would commence from February 18, 2004; Senior Secondary (Academic and Vocational) Examination would start from March 11, 2004; and Matric Examination would begin from March 12, 2004. All the Examinations would be conducted in Evening Session.

For the first time in the history of the Board of School

Education Haryana Identity Cards (I-cards) to the Supervisory Staff deputed on Centres will be issued during Annual Examinations-2004 for checking irregularities.

Supervisors would be required to attach these I-cards on their chest pockets so that the flying Squads could check identification of the supervisory staff.

The I-cards would be handed over to the Centre Superintendents through District Education Officers a day before the commencement of Examinations at the venue where Deputy Commissioners and Superintendents of Police would address them.

The I-cards would be given by Centre Superintendents to Chief Superintendents and Supervisors on the day of commencement of Examinations. The Supervisors deputed on examination duty would be required to paste their ticket size photographs on the I-cards.

The examination duty has been made compulsory and strict disciplinary action would be taken by the Education Department, Haryana against these who remained wilfully absent from the duty.

The duties of Supervisory Staff would not be changed and in case of emergency, appointment of Supervisors would be allowed only from the Reserve list provided by the Board.

The teachers contributing in containing the use of unfair means would be honoured. However, stern action would be taken by the Education Department Haryana against those teachers who found guilty of conniving in the use of unfair means.

The Board of School Education Haryana has decided to provide only one answer book to candidates of Matric and Senior Secondary (Academic/Vocational) Annual Examination-2004. The decision to this effect has been taken with a view to check copying and other irregularities. The candidates of Matric Annual Examinations would be provided 28-page answer book and the candidates of Senior Secondary (Academic & Vocational) would be provided 32-page answer book. All the candidates would be required to write their answers on these answer books only.

SECRECY BRANCH

Secrecy Branch gets the answer books of Senior Secondary/ Matric/Middle and Open School Examinations evaluated from the examiners and make available the award lists to the Computer cell. The details of the functions are as follows:-

(i) One collection centre at each district established for receiving answer books of all the examinations from the examination centres of the district.

(ii) The detail of estimated number of answer books centre-wise and subject-wise are prepared on the basis of centre statement received from the examination branches. Accordingly, the planning is made to dispatch the answer books subject-wise to each marking centre.

(iii) The sealed bundle of answer books collected/received at collection centres are sent to Board's office and further sent to marking centres according to the details already prepared. The Centre Superintendent attaches the Tag label with the Secrecy code of the examinations centre with the sealed bundle of answer books. The portion of Tag label on which secrecy code of the examination centre is cut and in place of it bag number is inserted on the sealed bundle and Tag label before the bundle of answers are sent to the marking centres.

(iv) Suitable number of single/Sub/Head examiners is appointed for marking work of answer-books of all the examinations of the Board. The examiners of Middle and Matric examinations March-2003 were appointed by the Computer Cell from the Staff Statement at random. The Computer Cell has to appoint examiners for all the examinations from the staff statement received from the schools for the ensuing examinations. The appointment of examiners are made seniority-wise and not on the basis of registrations according to the requirement.

(v) Two or three marking centres in the district for Middle and Matric examinations and one marking centre of Senior Secondary Certificate Examinations are established for getting the answer books evaluated previously. All the answer books of Middle and Matric examinations were marked at the marking centres and for Senior Secondary Certificate Examinations six subjects answer books were got evaluated at marking centres and rest of the answer-books were got evaluated by the examiners by sending the answer books at their home. But from this year all the answer books are to be marked at marking centres. Fictitious Roll Nos. were marked in place of original Roll Nos. Physics, Chemistry, Maths. And Biology subject till the last examinations but from this year these subjects of affixing fictitious Roll Nos. has been abolished. The answer books of these subjects are also to be marked at Marking Centres along with other subjects. The marking of all the examinations are to be done by spot marking at the marking centres except the vocational examinations for which marking shall be got done at home for some subjects.

(vi) The estimated amount of remunerations for marking the answer books at each marking centre is sent to the Controller for making payment to the examiners. The payment of the examiners who marked answer books at home are got made from the account branch later on.

(vii) The awards of practical subjects of private candidates of Middle and Matric examinations and the awards of all the practical subjects all candidates (Regular/Private) are sent to the Computer Cell.

(viii) The awards for the ensuing examinations are to be prepared by O.M.R. System and sent to the Computer Cell without stamping.

(ix) In addition to above, the answer books of the candidates involved in stray/UMC cases are got marked. The instructions are also set to the examiners.

The Board has enhanced the remuneration of paper setters who prepare Evaluation Instructions and Translations. For preparing Marking Schemes the remuneration has been enhanced to Rs.250/- from Rs.50/- per paper. For translation the remuneration has been enhanced to Rs.200/- from Rs.80/- per paper.

Computer: This Branch has the responsibility of doing all the work where computers are needed, particularly preparation of results etc.

This Board has become the first to provide scanned photographs of the candidates on their Roll Nos. / Hall Tickets, signature charts, check lists and certificates. This will totally eliminate impersonation as well as other malpractices.

Rechecking: The Board has decided to reduce the period of submission of forms for Rechecking from 40 days to 30 days from the day of declaration of results since the Board has been able to provide provisional certificates of candidates to all the schools at 3.00 p.m. on the day of declaration of results.

Accounts: This Branch makes all kinds of payments to supervisory staff, examiners and other related staff, salary payments, etc. All kinds of refunds and income-tax deductions etc. are also made by this branch. The work of the Accounts Branch is going to be fully computerized for which work has already started. This will make its functioning much more efficient.

General: All kinds of purchases etc. are the function of this Branch.

Maintenance: This Branch exercises control on construction work and maintenance of campus & houses. All vehicles, water works, in-house constructions & security works etc. are also under its charge.

Administration: All administrative matters & establishment of the Board comes under the jurisdiction of this Branch.

Legal : This Branch deals with legal matters and appointment of advocates for various court cases.

P.W.O. Cell : Press releases, contradictions and advertisements, etc. relating to all the Branches.

Publications and Printing: All kinds of printing work relating to the Board are managed by this Branch. Sale of books & various priced documents is also the responsibility of this Branch.

UNIVERSITIES

The Maharishi Dayanand University (MDU) at Rohtak, Kurukshetra University at Kurukshetra and Guru Jambheshwar University at Hissar are exclusively for the promotion of technical education and management studies in Haryana.

The Chaudhary Charan Singh Agriculture University (HAU) at Hissar being one of the biggest agriculture university in Asia is dedicated to agricultural education, research and development.

The National Dairy Research Institute (NDRI), Karnal has been upgraded to the status of 'deemed university'. NDRI provides excellent education in the field of dairy science and technology.

The distribution of total enrolment in colleges category-wise was Arts and Science colleges 91. 04 percent, Teacher Training colleges 1.11 percent, Medical Colleges 1.66 percent, Agriculture colleges 1.00 percent, Engineering Colleges 3.20 percent, Veterinary colleges 0.33 percent.

Physical education Colleges 0.59 percent and Oriental College 1.47 percent during the year 1998. The 10+2 education system consists of two components i.e. vocational and general education. The vocational program was introduced in 1983-84 in 24 institutions. Their number rose to 118 with seating capacity of 15440 in 1998-99.

The enrolment in these institutions was 16982 students in 1999-2000. In the year 2001-2002 Haryana's literacy rate stands at 68.59 % with males at 79.25 % and females at 56.31 %. Stress is being laid on the promotion of primary education so as to check the drop-out rate at lower level. A number of incentives are also given to the students to attract them to the educational institutes.

Haryana's main concern is to tackle the problem of illiteracy among its female population. The importance of education among girls and its over all impact on the welfare of children and community as a whole cannot be over ruled. Concessions and incentives for girls especially those belonging to backward/ EWS and scheduled castes have gone a long way in promoting female education.

Scheduled Caste/ EWS girls in primary, middle and high classes are being provided with free uniforms. Scheduled Caste/ EWS students are provided grants for books and stationery articles and are awarded scholarships and reimbursement of tuition fees. The Haryana Government is providing free education to the women up to graduation level and also in technical institutes.

In the year 2001-2002, Haryana had 30 Engineering Colleges, 29 Polytechnics, 12 MBA Colleges, 18 MCA Colleges, 3 B. Pharmacy Colleges, 76 Industrial Training Institutes (ITIs) and 116 Vocational educational institutes. Haryana also has three flying clubs, one each at Karnal, Hissar and Pinjore, where flying is taught, and from where private pilot license (PPL) can be obtained.

Chaudhary Charan Singh Agricultural University

Chaudhary Charan Singh Agricultural University, popularly known as HAU, is located in Hissar (Haryana). It was initially a campus of Punjab Agricultural University, Ludhiana, Punjab. In 1966, with the division of Punjab and Haryana, HAU became an independent land grant institution. Since then, HAU has become internationally known not only for its advances in high yielding grain and cotton varieties but also for its scenic campus.

The first Vice-Chancellor of HAU, Mr. A. L. Fletcher dedicated many years of his life in making HAU one of the best known institutions in Asia. His vision and efforts, as well as his proximity to the powers that be, led to an infusion of resources for creation of world class infrastructure, laboratories and other facilities on the main campus.

At present, the Chaudhary Charan Singh Agricultural University has seven colleges: College of Agriculture, College of Agricultural Engineering, College of Animal Sciences, College of Basic Sciences, College of Home Sciences, College of Sports and College of Veterinary Sciences.

In fact, HAU was the first institution of higher learning to create a separate college for sports in India. The University also has a research and training farm of over 3, 000 acres (about 1, 200 hectares) for faculty and students. The university recently annexed another 2, 000 acres for its seed operations. The University has a faculty of well over 1, 200 scientists most of whom have either been educated or trained abroad in their field of specialization.

HAU is also one of the three Indian universities to be a recipient of the recent World Bank project on Agricultural Human Resource Development.

The overall project is approximately US $240 million. Under the project, about 65 faculty members and deans/directors are scheduled to visit the United States, United Kingdom and other countries. The visitors will undergo three to four-and-a-half month trainings at selected universities in these countries. The project is currently under way (July 1998) and some faculty members have already started the trainings.

This university, which was earlier known as Hissar Agricultural University (HAU), was given its present name after Chaudhary Charan Singh, a former Prime Minister of India.

UNIVERSITIES AND HIGHER EDUCATION

Haryana has 29 universities and 299 colleges, including 115 government colleges, 88 govt-aided colleges and 96 self-finance colleges (c. Jan 2018).

Hisar has three universities: Chaudhary Charan Singh Haryana Agricultural University - Asia's largest agricultural university, Guru Jambheshwar University of Science and Technology, Lala Lajpat Rai University of Veterinary & Animal Sciences); several national agricultural and veterinary research centres (National Research Centre on Equines), Central Sheep Breeding Farm, National Institute on Pig Breeding and Research, Northern Region Farm Machinery Training and Testing Institute and Central Institute for Research on Buffaloes (CIRB); and more than 20 colleges including Maharaja Agrasen Medical College, Agroha.

Union Minister Ravi Shankar Prasad announced on 27 February 2016 that National Institute of Electronics and Information Technology (NIELIT) would be set up in Kurukshetra to provide computer training to youth and a Software Technology Park of India (STPI) would be set up in Panchkula's existing HSIIDC IT Park in Sector 23. Hindi and English are compulsory languages in schools whereas Punjabi, Sanskrit and Urdu are chosen as optional languages.

Sports

In the 2010 Commonwealth Games at Delhi, 22 out of 38 gold medals that India won came from Haryana. During the 33rd National Games held in Assam in 2007, Haryana stood first in the nation with a medal tally of 80, including 30 gold, 22 silver and 28 bronze medals.

The 1983 World-Cup-winning captain Kapil Dev is from Haryana. Nahar Singh Stadium was built in Faridabad in the year 1981 for international cricket. This ground has the capacity to hold around 25,000 people as spectators. Tejli Sports Complex is an Ultra-Modern sports complex in Yamuna Nagar. Tau Devi Lal Stadium in Gurgaon is a multi-sport complex.

Chief Minister of Haryana Manohar Lal Khattar announced the "Haryana Sports and Physical Fitness Policy", a policy to support 26 Olympic sports, on 12 January 2015 with the words "We will develop Haryana as the sports hub of the country."

Haryana is home to Haryana Gold, one of India's eight professional basketball teams which compete in the country's UBA Pro Basketball League.

Bibliography

Ali, M. Athar Ali: *The Mughal Nobility Under Aurangzeb*. Bombay: Asia Publishing House, 1968.

Begley, Wayne E.; Desai, Z.A. : *Taj Mahal - The Illumined Tomb*, University of Washington Press, 1989.

Chandra, Satish : *History of Medieval India*, New Delhi: Orient Longman, 2007.

Chaudhary, M.: *Partition and the Curse of Rehabilitation*, Calcutta, Bengal Rehabilitation Organization, 1964.

Choudhary, J. N. : *Divorce in India Society,* Jaipur, Rupo Books, 1988.

Dikshit, D.P. *Political History of the Chalukyas of Badami*. New Delhi: Abhinav, 1980.

Fairservis, Walter A.: *The Roots of Ancient India: The Archaeology of Early Indian Civilization*, New York, Macmillan, 1971.

Gambhirananda, S.: *Brahma Sutra Shamkar Bhasya,* Adavita Ashrama, Calcutta, 1977.

Gulbadan Begum : *Humayun Nama*, London 1902, Indian Reprint, Delhi, 1972.

Gurumurthy, S. : *Hindu Heritage, Assimilative, Not Divisive*, Vigil, Madras 1993.

Habib, Irfan : : *An Atlas of the Mughal Empire*, New York: Oxford University Press, 1982.

Heinsath, Charles: *Indian Nationalism and Hindu Social Reform*, Princeton, Princeton University Press, 1964.

Hujwiri, Al: *The Kashf al-Mahjub, the Oldest Persian Treatise on Sufism*, London, Luzac Press, 1959.

Hutton, J. H.: *Caste in India: Its Nature, Function and Origins*, London, Cambridge University Press, 1946.

Ibn Hasan, *The Central Structure of the Mughal Empire,* Macmillan, London, 1936.

Jain, Kailash Chand, *Lord Mahavira and His Times*, Saraswati Press, Delhi, 1974.

James, Lawrence: *The Rise and Fall of the British Empire*, St. Martin's, 1997.

Kalika Prasad Tiwari: *Foundations of Ancient Indian Culture*, Pointer Publishers, Delhi, 2001.

Lakshmanna, C.: *Caste Dynamics in Village India*, Nachiketa Publications, Bombay, 1973.

Lal, K.S. : *The Mughal Harem*. New Delhi: Aditya Prakashan, 1988.

Levy, Ruben: *The Social Structure of Islam*, Cambridge, 1957.

Mahalingam, T.V.: *Administration and Social Life under Vijayanagar*, Madras, University of Madras, 1969-75.

Moreland, W.H.: *From Akbar to Aurangzeb*, London, 1923.

Moynihan, E. : *Moonlight Garden: New Discoveries at the Taj Mahal*, Delhi, 2001.

Nanda, Ratish, : *Delhi : The Built Heritage - A Listing* , Indian National Trust for Art and Cultural Heritage, 1999.

Owen, Sidney J. : *The Fall of the Moghul Empire,* London, 1912,

Pelsaert, Francisco : *Jahangir's India*, Cambridge, 1925.

Prasad, Saksena Banarsi : *History of Shahjahan of Dihli,* Allahabad: The Indian Press, 1932.

Qaisar, Ahsan Jan : *Building Construction in Mughal India,* Delhi: Oxford University Press, 1989.

Qureshi, I. H.: *The Administration of the Mughals*. Lahore, 1944.

Rafiabadi, Naseem : *Islam and Sufism in Kashmir : Some Lesser Known Dimensions*, Sarup, Delhi, 2009.

Skelton, Robert : *The Indian Heritage: Court Life & Arts under Mughal Rule,* Delhi, 1982.

Stuart, C.: *The Art of Mughal India*. New York, 1964.

Tillotson, Giles : *The Tradition of Indian Architecture: Continuity, Controversy and Change since 1850,* Delhi, 1989.

Trimingham, J.: *Sufi Orders in Islam*, Oxford University Press, New York, 1998.

Index

❑❑❑

www.ingramcontent.com/pod-product-compliance
Ingram Content Group UK Ltd.
Pitfield, Milton Keynes, MK11 3LW, UK
UKHW042017290726
14061UKWH00001BB/33

9 789388 31872